CLOSE TO HOME

Women Reconnect Ecology, Health and Development

edited by
Vandana Shiva

Earthscan Publications Ltd, London

First published in the UK in 1994 by
Earthscan Publications Limited
120 Pentonville Road, London N1 9JN

Published in cooperation with Kali for Women, India

A catalogue record for this book is available from the British Library

ISBN: 1 85383 190 5

Cover photo by Jean-Luc Ray / Aga Khan Foundation. Cover design by Parallel Design, Inc. of Philadelphia, USA

Printed and boundby Capital City Press of Montpelier, USA

Earthscan Publications Limited is an editorially independent subsidiary of Kogan Page Limited and publishes in association with the International Institute for Environment and Development and the World Wide Fund for Nature.

Contents

Preface

The Seminar on 'Women, Ecology and Health: Rebuilding Connections', which has provided the basis for the material presented in this book, was held in Bangalore in southern India from July 17-22, 1991. It was jointly organised by the Dag Hammarskjold Foundation in Sweden and the Research Foundation for Science, Technology and Natural Resource Policy, Dehra Dun, India, and moderated by the Director of the latter, Vandana Shiva. It brought together 25 participants from seven South Asian and Southeast Asian countries and one participant from the United States. Both foundations are grateful to the participants for their valuable contribution to the seminar discussions and to the authors for the pains they have taken in thoroughly revising and updating their papers.

The basic idea behind the organisation of the Bangalore seminar was the conviction that, twenty years after 'the Environment' was placed on the international agenda, the time was ripe to take stock, from a gender perspective, of two decades of development in the environmental field. An important factor was the growing recognition that across the world women are rebuilding connections with nature and renewing the insight that what people do to nature directly affects them too; that there is, in fact, no insular divide between the environment and their own bodies and health.

Just as the seminar was the result of the combined efforts of the two organising foundations, this book is the result of a joint undertaking by the Dag Hammarskjold Foundation and Kali for Women. The collaboration which envisaged the simultaneous publication of the Seminar papers and discussions, was initiated at the Bangalore seminar itself and has since encompassed all aspects of the work, i.e., the selection of the material, revision, updating, editing, proof-reading and production. The Dag Hammarskjold Foundation has published the material as an issue of their journal, *Development Dialogue*.

An important consideration for this collaboration was the desire, shared by both the Dag Hammarskjold Foundation and Kali for Women, that the outcome of the seminar discussions be made available to as wide a readership as possible in the connected areas of development, gender and ecology, as well as among activists and non-governmental organisations working on these issues in the North and South. The collaboration itself between the two organisations, one in the North, the other in the South, one with a focus on development, the other on gender, highlighted yet another conviction held by both: the view that indigenous publishing is a crucially important part of intellectual and cultural development and international cooperation; it is hoped that this joint publishing effort will inspire similar undertakings by other organisations in this and other fields of endeavour.

Kali for Women   *Dag Hammarskjold Foundation*

Introduction
Women, Ecology and Health: Rebuilding Connections

Vandana Shiva

It is now twenty years since the 'environment' was put on the agenda of international concern with the Stockholm Environment Conference in 1972. The United Nations Conference on Environment and Development (UNCED) held in Rio de Janeiro in June 1992 marked the culmination of these two decades of environmentalism, enabling us to take stock of trends, to build on the most promising and lasting ones.

The global concern for planetary survival has moved from issue to issue in the last two decades. From desertification it shifted to acid rain, and the current preoccupation is the pollution of the atmospheric commons, symptomatised by the greenhouse effect and ozone depletion. The official environmental response has largely been one of offering technological and managerial fixes which, rather than addressing or solving the basic ecological problems, often create new ones. The search for technological fixes to the greenhouse crisis is an example of a cure which could be worse than the disease, destabilising the planet's life support systems and livelihoods in the Third World.

There is another response to the growing ecological crisis which comes from women engaged in the struggle for survival; because of their location on the fringes, and their role in producing sustenance, women from Third World societies are often able to offer ecological insights that are deeper and richer than the technocratic recipes of international experts or the responses of men in their own societies. There are two reasons for this.

Firstly, these responses come from cultures in which maintenance of life has been the civilising force; secondly, the gender division of labour, introduced or aggravated by the development process, has increasingly pushed women to work for the production of sustenance, while men have been drawn into military and profit-seeking activities.

In the post-UNCED era of 'global environmentalism', the two distinct processes outlined above continue to be at work for the identification of environmental problems and their solutions. In the dominant process, men in centres of economic and political power see the roots of the problem and the burden of solutions as lying outside themselves and their context. They begin with prescriptions for change in other places and by other people, often people and places that have been victims of the environmental consequences of decisions made in those very centres of power. Thus, the UN Conference on Environment and Development had a tendency to identify the South as the source of all environmental problems and the North, with its technology and capital, as the source of all environmental solutions.

The contributions in this volume illustrate a different process, one which re-locates the problem and begins with people's own lives. It connects global environmental issues with how people are affected, on a daily basis, in diverse local situations.

Earth body, human body: the continuity

The 'environment' in these papers is not an external, distant category; in Penny Newman's words, 'The "environment" for women in our communities is the place we live in and that means everything that affects our lives.'

Women's involvement in the environmental movement has started with their lives and with the severe threat to the health of their families. From the perspective of women, environmental issues are quite directly, and clearly, issues of survival. Ann Usher in her discussion on deforestation and AIDS explains, 'The Thai community forestry movement that emerged in the mid-1980s is not just a fight for rights over the forest. It is a fight for survival', a point Penny Newman makes in the context of toxic hazards.

Survival becomes the juncture connecting different movements and women in different locations. For women, health issues and environmental issues are related, as demonstrated most clearly in the first three contributions. Ann Usher shows how metaphorically and materially 'the condition of the human immune system weakened by AIDS shares many similarities with a degraded ecosystem like a dying forest.... Not only is the degraded forest unable to "perform" the functions that were once part of its nature, it becomes increasingly sensitive to unusual pressure from the outside.... Stresses that were once absorbed by the ecosystem without inflicting significant damage now cause devastation.'

Penny Newman shows the links between health problems and the pervasiveness of chemicals in our production systems. She also points out how white, male-dominated environmental organisations fail to see the interconnection between various issues—ozone depletion, acid rain, toxic wastes, pesticides—and to understand that they are actually one issue, the massive production of man-made chemicals by the petrochemical industry.

Mira Shiva further elaborates how health issues and environmental issues are one and the same. She demarcates diseases as arising from two conditions—deprivation of essentials or an excess of non-essentials; ecological erosion leads to the former, pollution to the latter. She further points out that no amount of drugs and doctors can create health if essentials are becoming more scarce due to ecological erosion, and non-essentials more pervasive due to consumerist life-styles, environmental pollution and the accumulation of waste.

Environmental problems become health problems because there is a continuity between the earth body and the human body through the processes that maintain life. This continuity also implies that the challenge of the re-production of nature and the challenge of the reproduction of society need to be addressed systemically. Reducing the problem of the reproduction of society, in the face of declining resources and declining access to resources, to a 'population problem' is another symptom of the tendency to treat people of other cultures, races and places not as human beings but as statistics to be manipulated. But behind the numbers being manipulated are real women with human rights and health needs. As Mira Shiva reports in her contribution:

For those involved in health work, population control policies have been a double tragedy, first because they failed to meet women's contraceptive needs and second because they eclipsed other necessary health care work.... Had those whose hearts bleed for the soaring population of India cared to listen, they would have recognised the needs to strengthen the hands of women early enough, educationally, economically and socially, so that they could be helped to make choices about conception and contraception.

An almost logical, and dangerous, extension of this is the subject of the contribution of the Forum Against Sex Determination and Sex Pre-selection (FASDSP): technologies that determine genetic characteristics in unborn foetuses. It addresses the political and ethical implications of the manipulation of women's bodies, either through invasive technologies or more subtly, to suit the gender bias of society. The patriarchal analogy of woman and nature is subverted through the women-ecology-health connections made in this volume, thus relocating the terms of the discourse through a redefinition of the human body, the earth body and the body politic.

People, their environment and their society are not separable by rigid and insular boundaries. The boundaries between them are porous and flexible, allowing interchange and influence. The unity here is not the uniformity of the fragmented atomism of Descartes and Hobbes. It rests on the continuity of life in its interconnectedness, there are subtle and complex connections between diseases of the human body, the decay of ecosystems and the break-down of civil society, just as there are connections in the search for health at all these levels.

As the 20th century closes, feminism is faced with two challenges: on the one hand there is the challenge posed by ecological disruption which threatens the very basis of life on this planet; on the other, there is a constant need to respond to, and transform, the patriarchal categories of definition and analysis that we have inherited.

The ecological challenge compels us to recognise connections and continuity within an organic, evolving, dynamic nature. A feminist response that is ecological must necessarily reactivate a conscious awareness of, and dialogue with, nature, lifting it out of its patriarchal definition as something passive and inert—a definition that has also been extended to women.

This separation between the natural and the human world was constructed simultaneously with the separation of mind from matter, and intellect from body. The exclusion of nature from culture and body from mind were used to essentialise gender in such a way that women were treated like nature, devoid of mind and thought, while men were constructed as distinct from the physical world, guided by reason alone and capable of complete intellectual transcendence of the body. How should we respond to these social constructions? The authors in this volume transcend the nature/culture dichotomy by recognising that the passivity and inertia of nature are a patriarchal construct and that the interconnectedness of women and nature can be one of creativity, life and intelligence. And, significantly, of resistance. This politics, based on nature taken as both female and intelligent, does not see liberation in severing the link between woman and nature, *but in recognising the necessary connection and continuity between the human and the natural*. It does not locate intelligence in the machine or artefact; rather, the ecological perspective acknowledges that some machines and artefacts in fact initiate disruption and imbalance. Chemical fertilisers were treated as total substitutes for, and an improvement of, the earth's fertility. Their use has led to soil, water and atmospheric pollution, and unhealthy plant growth, vulnerable to pests and diseases. An ecological perspective, therefore, emphasises the need to distinguish between artefacts, machines and other technological products on the basis of whether they interfere constructively or destructively with nature. It also raises fundamental questions about the political and social role of technology, by rejecting patriarchy's nature/culture dualism.

Separatism and the disintegration of the body politic

Separatism is patriarchy's favoured way of thought and action. There are many levels at which false separation creates conditions for ecological and social disruption and the marginalisation of women from the body politic. A neutral separatist boundary that women everywhere are challenging is between production and reproduction. This in turn derives from the basic dualism of nature/culture that characterises patriarchal paradigms, which exclude ecological contributions to the production of economic value. The externalisation of women's work and nature's work from dominant economic thought has allowed women's and nature's contributions to be used but not recognised. Nature's work is what ecological perceptions allow us to see.

'Nature' in this volume is also socially, culturally and politically constructed. Not only is it not outside economics and production, it is the basis of economic production. As Ann Usher and Vandana Shiva show in different ways, the 'virgin' view of nature necessarily goes hand in hand with the 'whore' view of what is not virgin nature. However, nature is neither 'virgin' nor 'whore', and ecology is not just conservation. Production happens in nature, in the home, in our daily lives, and is not limited by the artificial production and creation boundaries of patriarchal economics and scienc. The separation between production and reproduction, between innovation and regeneration, has been institutionalised to deny women and nature a productive role in the economic calculus. As all the contributors show, conservation must happen in the factory and in the city if total destruction is to be avoided. All the authors implicitly or explicitly question what is meant by 'production'. Gail Omvedt and Teresita Oliveros give accounts from India and the Philippines of how capitalist agriculture and industrial development have affected farmers, especially women farmers, and how they are engaged in struggles that simultaneously protect nature and their needs.

Gail Omvedt analyses the experience of peasant movements in the State of Maharastra in India, and shows how they are bringing issues of the reproduction of nature into agricultural production, thus changing the assumption about productivity and producers. The drought eradication campaign of the Mukti Sangharsh movement makes visible the environmental costs of sugarcane cultivation, and has led to the search for production systems which do not degrade land and water resources. This ecological perspective is also making women central to the search for sustainability, as captured in the slogan 'hirvi dharti, stri shakti, manav mukti' (green earth, women's power, human liberation), and in the experiments with *sita sheti*, small-scale, low-input agriculture production, mainly for consumption in the household.

Loreta Ayupan and Teresita Oliveros describe peasant women's direct action to resist their displacement by an industrial development project covering five provinces adjacent to Metro Manila. In a gesture of symbolic irony women in barrio Tartaria drove away surveyors who had come to survey land for a slaughterhouse and cemetery for the industrial zone: in the face of the expansion of this culture of death, peasant women in the Philippines 'are struggling to sustain and defend life by sacrificing their own'. For them, 'the survival of their families and communities is synonymous with the survival and preservation of the environment'.

The contributors also examine the notion of 'rights'. The concept of rights that derives from a fragmented view of nature is a notion that fails to protect either people's health or the health of ecosystems. Vandana Shiva points out how a system of rights derived from separation creates and protects property; Indira Jaising shows how existing jurisprudence is built around the protection of property, not the protection of life, and tells us how this jurisprudence militated against the delivery of justice to the victims of the Union Carbide disaster in Bhopal. She indicates that it is necessary to evolve a rights jurisprudence that protects people, their health, and ecosystems, while Vandana Shiva elaborates how notions of rights for the protection of property contradict rights to the protection of life, both in the case of human reproduction and of plant reproduction. Intellectual Property Rights (IPRs) are the ultimate Cartesian construct of a mind/body, culture/nature dualism, and perpetuate the evolution of ethics and law in the anti-ecological direction of 'separatist' rights to property which threaten farmers and women worldwide.

'Separatist' rights as embodied in IPRs, and in the negotiations at the General Agreement on Tariffs and Trade (GATT), have been identified as patriarchal projects by women activists of the South, rather than by feminist theorists of the North, indicating that our conventional notions of the separation of theory and action and of the primacy of the former need revision.

'Separatism' seems to be emerging as the contemporary expression of threatened patriarchal power, linked intimately to the global patriarchal project of forced integration into so called 'free markets'. 'Separatism' is appearing as a virus, infecting the body politic subjected to the rapid 'opening up' to global forces. Ethnic conflict, xenophobia, fundamentalism, and the rise of narrow nationalism are tearing apart the social fabric just as ecological destruction is tearing apart the web of life in nature. Integration as understood by global capitalist patriarchy is leading to disintegration because it is generating economic, social and cultural insecurities faster than people can identify the roots of these insecurities. Feeling the besieged 'other' in the global playing field of the market, and not being able to identify that field, members of diverse communities turn against each other, identifying their neighbours as the 'other' that poses a threat to their well-being and survival.

Since diversity characterises nature and society, the attempt to homogenise nature creates social and cultural dislocations, and the homogenisation of nature also becomes linked with the homogenisation of society. Ethnic and communal conflicts, which are, in part, a response to cultural homogenisation, are further aggravated by the process of development which dispossesses people, denies them control over resources and degrades ecosystems.

Rita Sebastian chronicles the devastation of Sri Lanka by the ethnic conflict which has been inflamed in recent years by rapid integration into world markets through free trade zones, and gigantic projects such as Mahaweli to supply power to the export industry.

The accelerated Mahaweli development programme in Sri Lanka is an example of development policies that ignore both human and environmental factors and a long-term perspective. Building dams across Sri Lanka's longest river, the programme deforested and changed the contours of vast areas of land, at the same time displacing thousands of families, largely peasants. These peasants were then resettled in parts of the north-central and eastern provinces. The resettlement policy led to a dramatic change in demographic patterns of the eastern province in particular, altering a previously balanced ethnic composition in favour of the majority Sinhalese community and thereby increasing ethnic tensions.

It would be wrong to assume that 'separatist' views only infect the body politic in the South. Yugoslavia is an indication that this is a global phenomenon.

We see the spread of violence as the culmination of patriarchal projects in which the potential for death and destruction is far greater than for the sustenance and reproduction of life. Superficial ideas of what development should be have led to the rise of fundamentalism, terrorism and communalism*, which further threaten life and peace. The feminist response to violence against women, against nature and against people in general attempts to make the production and sustenance of life the organising principle of society and economic activity. Whether it is the technological terrorism of Union Carbide in Bhopal, or the terrorism of racism, fundamentalism and communalism in Europe, Pakistan, India and Sri Lanka, we see a culture of violence and death extinguishing a culture in which life is generated, protected and renewed. It is in reclaiming life and recovering its sanctity that women of our region search for their liberation and the liberation of their societies.

Rebuilding connections

A common criticism levelled at ecological feminist approaches to the current crisis, is that of 'essentialism'; relating environmental issues to women in a specific way is seen as an 'essentialist' world view. Yet the charge itself emanates from a paradigm that splits part from whole, fragments and divides, and either sees the part as subjugating the whole (reductionism) or the whole as subjugating the parts—in other words, essentialising both.

There are, however, other paradigms in which the whole and the part carry each other—the part is not separate from the whole, but its embodiment, in flux, in dynamism, in change. Quantum theory is probably the best illustration of how parts embody wholes, because quantum subsystems which have

---

* In the Indian subcontinent, communalism refers in particular to social and political relations between the majority Hindu community and Muslim, Sikh and other minorities.

been part of a system do not behave as individual, unconnected fragments on separation, but have connected histories in spite of separation. The famous Einstein-Podolsky-Rosen paradox raises major philosophical issues related to this non-reductionist, non-hierarchical relationship between parts and wholes. The whole is not external to the part in all paradigms of 'nature' and 'society'. This is what David Bohm is pointing to through his concept of enfoldment and the implicit order in which the whole is enfolded in the part and unfolds through it.

A second aspect of the charge of essentialism is that it comes from a view that treats nature as inert and passive, and without intrinsic value. By failing to recognise nature's diversity, its regenerative capacity and its production of life, this view essentialises all production into human or technological intervention.

Another charge of essentialism comes from those who see difference as so 'essential' that it makes solidarity and commonality impossible. This again is based on the patriarchal paradigm of 'sameness'; if people, things, organisms are different, then the assumption is that they can have no relationship and no overlap. This leads to a solipsism that interprets relating and connecting as sameness and the argument that the search for common ground for women's actions and concerns is essentialising the category 'woman'. There is, however, no essentialism involved in partnerships, in solidarity, in symbiosis. Women acting together in spite of their diversity, is not equivalent to the essentialising of woman as a uniform category. Yet another common criticism of reconnecting with nature is that it involves a return to the past. This criticism arises from externalising nature in space and time; connections then imply a 'return' to another time, another place. If, however, our perceptions are ecological, then nature is the complex web of processes and relationships that provide the conditions for life. In this view, nature is not external, and it is not spatially and temporally separated from our being. Essential ecological processes that maintain life cannot be treated as part of the world-view of technological obsolescence. The moment we accept conditions for life as obsolete aspects of a primitive past, we invite death and destruction. In fact, it is this chrono-colonisation, or temporal colonisation, of living processes based on false and artificial constructions of 'traditional', 'modern', 'post-modern', as if they are in a linear temporal hierarchy of the past, the present and the future, which underlie the subjugation of nature and women. This colonisation of life cycles and time separates production from reproduction, as Vandana Shiva analyses in her paper on 'The Seed and the Earth'. The separation of the conditions of life from ourselves and our economic and scientific activity, and the location of these conditions in the past, are a major cause of the ecological destruction of ecosystems and of our bodies.

Through these contributions we attempt to reconstitute both 'woman' and 'nature', and to show that nature as the ecological web of life is not out there in space and time: it is us.

Across the world, women are rebuilding connections with nature, and renewing the insight that what we do to nature, we do to ourselves. There is no insular divide between the environment and our bodies. Environmental hazards are also health hazards, as was so brutally revealed in Bhopal and at Love Canal. Environmental hazards are also health hazards in food systems. Pesticides do not merely pollute fields, they end up polluting our bodies. Destruction of biodiversity does not merely impoverish nature, it impoverishes tribal and peasant societies. These links exist in the real world even though they have been denied by fragmented and divided worldviews. Beginning with women's experiences, analysis and actions we will rebuild the connections between ecology and health, for a more holistic approach to the contemporary crisis of survival.

After the Forest
AIDS as Ecological Collapse in Thailand

Ann Danaiya Usher

Introduction

Current research suggests that there are about 500,000 people infected with the AIDS virus in Thailand. AIDS is spreading rapidly among people in almost every walk of life and, according to one conservative estimate, two million people, or about three per cent of the current Thai population, will be carrying this apparently fatal disease by the year 2000.[1] The actual number will almost certainly be higher than this.

Nothing like this has ever happened in modern Thai history. Since 1987 we have been trying to come to grips with what is turning into an epidemic of unspeakable proportions; not merely learning to accept it as a permanent, tragic fixture of social reality, to follow its epidemiology, to guess its magnitude at any given time—but to understand something more profound about the phenomena that have allowed AIDS to take root so rapidly and so violently in Thailand, and to trace the politics, attitudes and structures that are ensuring its unhindered spread.

This essay diverges from conventional ways of thinking that often focus on a single dimension of the epidemic—AIDS as a public health problem, or a reflection of racial or sexual or class discrimination; AIDS as a function of pharmaceutical politics, or a political priority in competition, say, with military spending; AIDS as an issue of population control, the sex industry or tourism. AIDS is related to all of these things, but each seems to illuminate only one face of this many-headed beast.

This essay attempts to look at AIDS as a phenomenon embedded in, and inseparable from, other social realities. My own involvement in the Thai environmental movement causes me to focus attention on the connections between AIDS and the ecological crisis in Thailand. For anyone who has studied either of these, a number of parallels become immediately obvious. There is, for example, the sense of urgency and the pressing need for action to reverse, or at least stabilise, the deteriorating situation. Just as the number of people being infected by the AIDS virus rises each day, so ecosystems that took thousands of years to evolve are being fragmented and degraded in one human generation. The sense of crisis is heightened by the apparent irreversibility of the damage being done. Another obvious parallel exists at the level of the system—the individual human body with its internal regulatory processes on one hand, and ecosystems in nature, on the other, be they forests, swamps, rivers or fields. Immune deficiency caused by AIDS, which triggers gradual disintegration of the body's defence·mechanisms, mirrors erosion of the ecosystem which destroys the natural capacity to regenerate.

On closer examination, however, other more complex connections begin to emerge. There is, for example, the cultural fragmentation that occurs 'after the forest'; of communities that once depended for food, clothing, medicine, shelter, and tools, as well as spiritual sustenance, on intact ecosystems. The increasing centralisation of the state, and the intensification of resource use for industrial development, is causing the gradual erosion not only of natural resources but also of people's customary rights to land, cultural integrity, local knowledge and sense of belonging. For people living in a weakened environment, the 'goods and services' that were derived to a significant extent from nature must now, increasingly, be replaced by the market. But purchasing food or drugs or cultural commodities (through television, for example) demands the exchange of items that have the equivalent outside market value, forcing people either to extract more and more from the ecosystem, or to leave the village altogether. In the extreme case, when nature is so degraded that it can no longer provide, one of the only remaining local resources in the community that has value on the market is the bodies of the young. In those places where adolescent women—and, to a lesser extent, men—leave home to sell their labour in the sex industry, AIDS, which appears to have infected a huge proportion of the country's half-million prostitutes, has become a physical manifestation of political dispossession.

Another parallel between the AIDS crisis and deforestation—which will be the main focus of this paper—can be discerned in the way that society perceives the problem. There is an overriding tendency to stigmatise the most disadvantaged, placing blame for the problem on the victims. These prejudices are reflected in commonly-used terms like 'illegal sex workers' and 'forest encroachers', who are fingered as the cause, respectively, of AIDS and the forest crisis. One rarely hears, for example, that the government is concerned about 'illegal sex buyers' or 'encroaching loggers' who move into forests that local people have depended on for centuries. Instead, official solutions tends to criminalise the victims (who are, in any case, not in a position to change their way of life at will) with regulations that are impossible to enforce. Based on a skewed, reductionist analysis, these efforts have sometimes been ineffective, and often counter-productive. Forest laws tend to intensify pressure on villagers either to push farther into intact forests, or to abandon the rural areas in search of employment in the industrial sector. Meanwhile, the state's initial attempts to regulate AIDS have offered little solace for infected people, encouraging them instead to go underground to escape state surveillance, thereby making the epidemic more difficult to monitor and control. Both the existing policies and laws, and new legislation being passed in response to the crises, have virtually guaranteed the exacerbation of these processes.

In response to draconian, and often counter-productive measures, there has emerged an atmosphere of debate and critical discussion within civil society that has had an impact up to the policy level. A growing network of landless villagers, supported by the students' movement, environment activists and university scientists, has blocked a number of key forest-destroying projects and laws since the mid-1980s. This movement has turned the deforestation crisis in Thailand into a major national issue, and effectively exposed the myth that only the educated middle class care about the environment. Indeed, in hundreds of instances around the country, it is farmers and forest dwellers who, in fighting to protect their ways of life, have been in the front lines of battles to defend the integrity of ecosystems.

In a similar vein, doctors, social scientists, and activists—working on everything from women's and children's rights, prostitution and public health, to slums and rural development issues—challenged the government's initial denial of the AIDS epidemic and subsequent tendency to persecute the victims. From 1987, when few people in the country even knew what AIDS was, Thailand today has a government which is—largely as a result of pressure from these citizens' groups—one of the most open about AIDS in the region. AIDS continues to spread rapidly, and inordinate blame is still placed on women as transmitters of the virus via the sex industry, but several particularly discriminatory measures have been stopped or reversed. While this may not at first seem to signify much progress, the insistent denial of the epidemic by other governments in the region underlines how important this basic openness is.

There are enough parallels between AIDS and deforestation to make the relationship significant, if not essential, to the understanding of the spread of this disease in Thailand. Whether the ecological crisis is a cause—or the cause—of the epidemic, I cannot yet say. I am not even sure that it is necessary to answer this question. I believe it is enough, for now at least, to trace how the processes of degradation in the human body, the community and the ecosystem are linked physically, politically, and metaphorically, each reflecting and shedding light on the others.

Finally, this paper comes out of my personal bewilderment about the fate of women in Thailand who are being infected with AIDS, but appear to be insufficiently armed to protect themselves. The situations of young country girls working in the sex trade, risking their lives each day to earn money to send home, and that of the wives and lovers of male clients who become unknowingly infected, would appear to be very different. For the prostitute, AIDS infection has become a hazard of the job against which she can, in theory (if she knows about condoms and the customer is willing to use them), defend herself. Obviously, the use of the shield will also protect her and her clients against possible infection with AIDS and other sexually-transmitted diseases. The woman who is infected at home is in some senses a more innocent victim. The fatal virus that her husband may have picked up during an evening spree endangers not only her life, but the life of her un-born children, through possible perinatal infection. As different as these situations are, the fact of AIDS links both kinds of women in the most inti-mate of ways, forcing us to explore these links and fundamentally re-examine our attitudes towards sexuality.

Urban middle class value systems of the pre-AIDS age defined a woman's sexuality in terms of her relationship to men. She was respectable if she kept her virginity until marriage, and she was looked down upon if she did not. Prostitution, being both illegal and immoral, was nevertheless seen to be a 'necessary' evil that protected the respectability of the majority of women. While their husbands bought sexual relations with any number of partners with cash or favours, a woman's sexuality belonged exclusively to one man. A woman's social survival in the pre-AIDS age involved shielding herself from her sexuality—and therefore, from self-knowledge.

But what will women teach their daughters about survival in the age of AIDS? Clearly, the answer involves something much more profound than instruction in the use of condoms. *The answer lies somewhere in the ability of women to regain self-knowledge.* Barring the discovery of a miracle cure or vaccine, both of which appear to be distant possibilities at best, this knowledge could be a key to stemming the spread of AIDS in Thailand. Here again, the links between the social phenomenon of this growing AIDS epidemic and the ecological crisis within which it is taking place may illumi-nate some of the issues women must face. Just as the environmental move-ment is responding to the forces that would fracture living systems on which people's lives depend, women must also resist society's attempts to impose divisive values and definitions. As communities reclaim local wisdom that has been systematically devalued in the process of industrialisation, per-haps women can likewise reclaim and re-build their own self-knowledge.

'First, the forest died ...'

I begin this essay where some of these ideas began: in the spring of 1989. As part of former Prime Minister Chatichai Choonhavan's effort to convince a sceptical public of his concern for the welfare of people living beyond the Bangkok Metropolitan area, the premier instituted a short-lived tradition of regional Cabinet meetings. The first one, which took place in the south of the country, escaped the notice of almost everyone except local chambers of commerce which hoped to clinch a few deals during the high-level visit. The second was much livelier, its highlight being the arrival of thousands of landless villagers, who converged on the northeastern capital of Khon Kaen, demanding land rights.

By the time the third and final of these 'mobile meetings' came to the northern city of Chiang Mai in the spring of 1989, people had become quite accustomed to the idea. Much to the anxiety of the local police and military who were used to strict security for travelling VIPs, the easy-going PM seemed to welcome the chaos and excitement. The days leading up to the event were filled with all manner of activities as befitted such a rare occurrence as the visit of the Prime Minister. Most dynamic among these were the seminars and planning meetings, protests and demonstrations of numerous groups of villagers eager to make the most of this opportunity to influence policy, or at least have grievances heard directly by the policy-makers.

One of the groups was from Huay Kaew village in Chiang Mai's Sankamphaeng District. The villagers had been engaged for several months in a fight for the right to community management of a 2.5 square kilometre area of forest. The wife of a local Member of Parliament had rented the 'degraded' land ostensibly to plant a mango orchard. There were rumours that a hill resort would follow. Local people, however, living without land rights in this government-owned forest land had a very different perception. The area contained plenty of very old trees, and myriads of other plants and animals on which they depended. The forest also regulated the flow of water into their rice fields through Muang Fai, traditional irrigation canals, an 'ecological service' that ended abruptly as the concessionaire started clearing the land, clogging streams and fields with silt and forest debris.

It is unclear today whether the public marches and private discussions with the premier's advisers during the mobile Cabinet meeting had a direct and positive impact. The following December, however, after a prolonged political battle, the area of natural forest around Huay Kaew village became the first officially recognised community forest in Thailand. This has not guaranteed the long-term legal right of local people as there is still no community forest law. They even fear that the MP's wife is preparing to return with her tractors and mango saplings. However, Huay Kaew became a milestone in the Thai environmental movement, setting an important precedent for future forest debates.

Another group of villagers whose presence could not be ignored by the visiting ministers were from Chiang Muan district in the adjacent province of Phayao. They had got wind of the Cabinet's plans to give the final go-ahead for a large irrigation dam across the Yom River—the last of the four main tributaries of Thailand's lifeline, the Chao Phya River, that still remains free-running. The Kaeng Sua Ten project was, and remains, Step One in a massive water diversion scheme that would pump water from the mouths of two tributaries of the Mekong River, the Kok and the Ing, in the far north. This would be channelled into the Chao Phya basin many hundred kilometres southward, occasionally uphill, through a series of canals, tunnels and several dams, to fill up the reservoirs of two ageing hydro dams that are chronically short of water, the Bhumibhol and the Sirikit: more big dams to compensate for the failures of existing big dams.

Fearing that their agricultural land and forests would be flooded, the local people vigorously opposed the plan. What little information they received from government authorities suggested that only three villages would be inundated by the reservoir. As it turned out, the gaily-coloured map presented by Royal Irrigation Department officials to the mobile Cabinet was a complete forgery, the real number of settlements inside the flood zone area being 14, not three. In any case, the protests of some 6,000 people in Phayao and the arrival of several hundred in Chiang Mai to meet the ministers was enough to cause the project to be shelved for the time being. Kaeng Sua Ten became the second of four big dams in Thailand to be cancelled due to public protest since 1986.[2]

Many groups were given time to address the premier personally. In addition to villagers from Chiang Muan and Huay Kaew, there were delegations of hill-tribe people, representatives of the 'For Chiang Mai' group seeking a ban on high-rise condominiums, as well as people speaking on problems of intravenous drug use, uncontrolled tourism, expanding slums, prostitution and AIDS.

It was in the midst of the commotion surrounding these events that I first had the opportunity to meet Oranong Phaowattana, known to most as 'Khru (teacher) Noi', one of a rare breed of village headwomen.[3] Khru Noi had come from Chiang Rai province to talk about the need for 'real development' in the villages. She would explain to the Prime Minister that this was the only way they could hope to slow the deluge of young girls and boys who leave each year to work in the sex industry.

Khru Noi knew a lot about the sex industry, but at the time she knew very little about AIDS. This was early 1989, and most people still had only the vaguest understanding of, or interest in, a disease that was portrayed in government propaganda and much of the media as a problem of drug addicts and homosexuals. Already, though, the rates of infection were climbing among prostitutes and their clients, and there were some indications that pregnant mothers might also be catching the virus. Khru Noi said they had enough to worry about, and AIDS seemed so complicated. I pressed her all the same: How much did the young people know about AIDS before they left home to start working as prostitutes? Would they go anyway, even if they understood the risks? What would they do if they became infected with AIDS? How would their families cope when the main bread-winners were stricken with a fatal disease? How would rural northern communities respond when their children started coming home dying?

Khru Noi listened to my questions and then fell silent for a few moments.

She sighed, and finally spoke:

'First, the forest died ...', she said.

Khru Noi talked about how the forest once formed the fabric of people's lives, providing everything from food and shelter to spiritual meaning. But gradually, the forest began to disappear. The companies started coming in and taking out the big trees. Local people were confused at first, but lacking any legal right to the land and sensing the cutting was inevitable, many of them hired themselves out to log for the timber merchants. At the same time, others were squeezed off their low-land farms to make way for dams, roads and expanded rice or cash crop cultivation, and followed the timber roads into the uplands.

She explained that northern people used to derive almost everything from the forest. As the market economy reached the village and values from 'the outside' became more dominant, people started consuming more—buying radios, TVs, motorcycles, refrigerators. At one time, she said, the farmers could buy what commodities they needed with cash earned by selling local products. But as the forest died, so sources of cash income dried up. As expectations grew, so they became increasingly difficult to fulfil. Gambling, drinking, drug addiction became prevalent. Lacking official land title, many people found it impossible to acquire credit from banks, and were forced to seek loans at exceedingly high interest rates from local moneylenders. Unable to pay off debts, farmers were faced with the prospect of losing their land.

In this context, said Khru Noi, the young people's labour became a commodity with significant value on the outside market. The men mostly went off to work in industrial factories and some of the women entered the sex industry. In the early years, children were frequently tricked into prostitution by conniving agents, or sold by their parents—sometimes unknowingly—who were desperate for cash. But increasingly young women left on their own, often having a strong sense of pride and duty to help the family. They were tempted by the pull of the big city, the attraction of the bright lights and excitement, the glamour shown through the media. The exodus was accelerated by many other factors as well, such as the Vietnam War and, later, the growth of tourism. The stories told by older sisters and brothers arriving home in nice clothes with pockets full of cash made the younger ones even more curious. The culture came to adjust to the economic necessity, she said. Women who had worked for a time as prostitutes in cities in Thailand or abroad, came back to the north, married and settled down. They bought their families houses that were bigger and more colourful than their neighbours'; they donated money to enlarge and beautify local temples. They supported younger siblings' education, and paid off debts to keep the land.

This is how it came about, said Khru Noi. But this was early 1989, and she could not guess what would happen when the daughters—and the sons—started coming home dying of AIDS.

Today it is still unclear how rural culture in northern Thailand and the other regions will respond to the coming waves of death. Random and selective screening show that the rate of infection is sky-rocketing, but the actual number of people on record who have developed symptoms and died is still quite low. It is certain, however, that while the sex trade is the engine of the epidemic, it is not only prostitutes who carry the virus. It has spread in the north and elsewhere among sex workers and clients, among intravenous drug users and their sex partners, among heterosexual and homosexual lovers, husbands and wives, and finally perinatally to the children. In retrospect, given the experiences mapped out in the United States and countries of Africa, the Caribbean and Western Europe during the 1980s, the path of the disease was predictable. But no-one imagined how ferociously AIDS would take hold in Thailand.

The spread of AIDS: 1987 to 1991

1987 was Visit Thailand Year, the Thai government's all-out effort to put the country on the map for fun-and-sun-seeking vacationers. Over the course of that year, tourism became the country's number one foreign exchange earner, surpassing rice and textiles. Visit Thailand Year was a veritable public relations orgy, an extravaganza of shameless commercialism. Glossy posters depicted everything up for sale—from spotless white beaches to luscious tropical jungles, from colourful cultural events to beautiful Thai women 'wai'-ing in the traditional posture of greeting. The most infamous attraction, of course, was the sex, though the Tourism Authority of Thailand continues to deny vigorously critics' accusations of promoting sex tourism. TAT has some justification in this claim, as none of the literature referred outright to prostitution. But the visions of beaches and attractive beckoning women, sub-titled with phrases like 'the land of smiles welcomes you', were extremely suggestive. The tourism authority certainly never took a public stand against sex tourism during that year.

Two Thai AIDS carriers were identified between 1984 and 1986, both homosexual men who had apparently picked up the virus during visits abroad. This fact, coupled with news from New York and San Fransisco, focused much of the local concern about AIDS during Visit Thailand Year on the four million-odd foreigners who were expected to arrive in the country. A memorable street theatre protest by a women's group reflected this concern. It involved three people in flamboyant costumes—a prostitute wearing a mini-skirt chained to a fat Thai pimp and a very blonde tourist in bermuda shorts with dollar bills spilling out of his pockets. The pickets read: 'Thailand No Sexland', 'AIDS Carriers Go Home'.

Indeed, 1987 appears to be the year AIDS tightened its grip. And the Visit Thailand Year hysteria certainly facilitated this, but not necessarily because foreign sex tourists were infecting Thai prostitutes, as many of us feared. Rather, in the government's frantic efforts to protect the 'holy cow' that tourism had become, news about AIDS was played down or censored. Results of the little testing that was being done were kept secret, the public was kept in the dark about the dangers of this new and fatal virus, and a negligible budget was provided to the Ministry of Public Health. In response to criticism, then Prime Minister Prem Tinsulanonda dismissed AIDS as being 'just like any other disease'. Delighted by the bulging national (and private) coffers, his government extended the international promotion campaigns of Visit Thailand Year for an additional six months. Nineteen eighty seven became the longest year in the history of the world.

Meanwhile, AIDS was quietly spreading inside the country among people, mostly poor people, who had little contact with foreigners. Thailand emerged from this period with the seeds of an epidemic firmly planted.

Would a massive public education blitz in that crucial year have made any difference? Perhaps, and perhaps not. Thailand's national character profile already made the country a perfect host for the AIDS virus: firstly, Thailand has one of the world's most infamous sex industries, but it remains a matter of heated debate how many prostitutes the industry employs at any given time—in Thailand or abroad. Because prostitution is illegal in the country, it is difficult to obtain reliable statistics. I am not aware of any attempts to guess the numbers of people, mostly women, who work as prostitutes outside Thailand, for example in Japan, Macao, Hong Kong, Singapore and Western Europe.

In Thailand, however, estimates vary from an official figure of as low as 86,000 to unofficial numbers ranging from 500,000 to two million. The high-end estimate, which comes from Sapphasit Khumpraphan of the Centre for Protection of Children's Rights who conducted a province-by-province survey, includes 800,000 child prostitutes.[4] Mechai Viravaidhya of the Population and Community Development Association is one who strongly objects to Sapphasit's claim. He has pointed out that with 2.5 million Thai girls between the ages 13 and 16, such a figure implies that one in three Thai girls is a prostitute.[5] And the overall estimate of two million suggests that one in every five Thai women aged 13 to 29 is a sex worker. Dr Weerasit Sittitrai of Chulalongkorn University and doctors at the Thai Red Cross estimate more conservatively that there may be about 200,000 prostitutes in the country, which represents 2.4 per cent of Thai women aged 15 to 29.[6] Another prominent Thai AIDS activist, Jon Ungphakorn, has suggested a figure between these two: 500,000.[7]

Contrary to the conventional understanding outside Thailand, the sex industry is not dominated by foreign clients. It serves Thai men, both single and married. It has become a social norm for many men in all economic classes to frequent 'entertainment establishments', be they brothels or tea houses, cocktail lounges or massage parlours, by-the-hour motels or private member clubs.

Secondly, being a heroin-exporting country with ready access to the drug, Thailand has a huge user community: an estimated 200,000 people, mostly concentrated in the capital. For many reasons, users usually share their needles. Heroin is illegal and possession of a syringe or other injection equipment can be used by police as grounds for arrest. The drug often finds its way into prisons where both equipment and the means of keeping it clean are in short supply. Of late, heroin use appears to be spreading like wild fire among young men in some rural areas, for reasons that are still difficult to understand.*

Another factor that has helped to make Thailand a 'perfect host' for AIDS is the homosexual community. Gay western men swear that outside of San Fransisco, Thailand is the one place in the world where homosexuals are, if not fully accepted, then generously tolerated. Indeed, 'gay-bashing' is quite unheard of. Numerous public personalities in Thai society have been gay—from politicians to movie stars to pop singers and famous intellectuals. As a result, unlike nearby countries such as Korea, Taiwan, Singapore and Malaysia where homophobic sentiments run high, there is a flourishing homosexual community in Thailand. And because of the work of gay activists, Thai homosexuals may be among the most well-informed about AIDS.

Tragically, the same cannot be said about the rest of society. Here are a few examples of the numbers: blood screening of intravenous heroin users in detoxification clinics run by the Bangkok Metropolitan Administration indicated that, in 1987, one per cent of those who sought treatment were infected with HIV. By January 1988, the numbers of infected addicts catapulted to 15 per cent and in September of the same year, to 43 per cent.[8] Ministry of Public Health screenings of prisoners also revealed high infection rates in some jails.

At about the same time, Dr Vicharn Vithayasai of the University Hospital in Chiang Mai was carrying out surveys of sex workers in the northern capital. He found that there was a less than one per cent infection rate. By mid-1989, his screening programme indicated that 16 per cent of 'high class' prostitutes who receive few clients per day were infected. For those women at the lower end of the economic scale who had intercourse with 10 men per day, between 44 and 72 per cent were carrying HIV. Moreover, Dr Vicharn's study of men in the 'general population'—derived by screening voluntary blood donors, as well as men who sold their blood to blood banks—

---

* Intravenous drug use is one of the main vectors through which AIDS has taken hold in the Thai population. Its role in the epidemic deserves far more attention than I am able to give in this article.

showed that between two and six per cent of the sample groups carried the AIDS virus.[9]

By the end of 1990, one of the most comprehensive AIDS surveys conducted on new army recruits in the northern region suggested the disease was still spreading with a vengeance. It involved total screening of 20- to 24-year-old men, mostly poor youths from rural areas. (Families with enough money can usually bribe their sons' way out of the compulsory two-year military service.) Dr Thaweesak Nopkesorn of the Phitsanuloke province army hospital reported in December that among the more than 1,000 young men recruited in the last half year, infection rates ran as high as 10 per cent in the major northern centres, such as Chiang Mai and Chiang Rai. Six months later, the proportion of men carrying AIDS from these same areas jumped to 14 per cent, and continues to climb.[10]

Not surprisingly, young men are transferring the virus to their lovers and wives, who then infect their children. It is estimated that in 1990, 3,000 babies were born to Thai women infected with AIDS.[11] As 30 per cent of such children usually contract AIDS perinatally, about 1,000 of these babies will probably fall sick, while the rest will remain healthy but are likely to become orphans eventually. One report suggests that as many as 10,000 babies were born with AIDS during 1992. As of June 1991, nation-wide sample surveys conducted by the government revealed that rates of infection were 24 per cent of brothel prostitutes, eight per cent of males attending state clinics for sexually transmitted diseases, and one per cent of women attending government ante-natal clinics.[12] By 1992, several northern provinces were registering up to 6 per cent sero-positivity among pregnant women.

The current figures are grim, and the projections are worse. One World Health Organization report for the Thai government predicted that there will be 1.6 million AIDS carriers in Thailand by the end of 1995. This was based on a scenario in which rates of infection would gradually tail off by the mid-1990s as a result of successful education campaigns and behaviour change.

Another study conducted by the Population and Community Development Association in cooperation with epidemiologists at WHO offers 'conservative' and 'realistic' scenarios for the course of AIDS in Thailand up to the year 2000. Assuming 200,000 to 240,000 Thais were infected at the end of 1990, the model predicts that there could be between two and six million AIDS carriers by the turn of the century, depending on how soon the epidemic peaks.[13]

Despite these obvious trends, initial government information campaigns were desperately slow and often mis-targeted. The first posters to emerge from the health ministry depicted hooded skeletons with A I D S written in squiggly letters. Later a syringe with blood dripping from the needle was added to the horrifying image. In response to continued complaints and criticism of this doom-and-gloom approach to public education, the focus shifted to warnings for men thinking of going to a prostitute. In the early 1990s, the message started targeting women directly—one poster showing a pregnant woman sitting in a rocking chair, worrying about the baby's health, and what her child will do once she develops full-blown AIDS.

We could have guessed it in 1987. People like Dr Vicharn knew it by 1989. Today it is an absolute certainty that the notion of high-risk groups has very limited usefulness in the Thai context. It serves no practical purpose to point fingers at the drug users or the prostitutes. If there is one thing AIDS has shown us, it is that societies cannot be easily compartmentalised. A man may for a brief time have a male lover and then return to his wife. A person might become addicted to heroin and use the drug for two months or years, and then stop. A university student might go carousing with his friends and later join the monkhood, carrying the virus with him. A girl from Chiang Rai might go to work in Hat Yai or Singapore and make enough money that she never enters the sex industry again. After a few years she might, as is often the case, return to her village, get married and raise a family. A Bangkok bar boy might make a living by entertaining gay men, but during his days off spend time with his girlfriends, or later marry and have children.

AIDS is a disease of the whole, however hard we try to separate and point fingers, to quarantine and ostracise and amputate. The whole of society is vulnerable to this epidemic, and no healing will take place unless it is a healing of the whole.

The body

No-one has ever died of AIDS. People infected with the human immune deficiency virus fall prey to ailments that a normal healthy person might barely notice. People with AIDS die of tuberculosis, they die of cancers and pneumonia, they die of internal haemorrhaging, they die because wounds inflicted from a bump or a fall never heal but just get worse. This is why healthy people, unaware they are carrying all manner of germs and viruses, are more dangerous to AIDS patients than the reverse. A person with AIDS can die from a common cold.

AIDS is a syndrome in which the body's immunity goes berserk. Simple things like walking or digesting food become exhausting chores. Basic processes like maintenance of body temperature, chemical balances and blood cell production that healthy people take for granted, malfunction or cease to function as the natural defence system, which normally regulates these internal processes, is weakened by AIDS. But it is not AIDS that ultimately kills. Vulnerable to the slightest infection or stress, the body eventually dies because it has lost the capacity to protect itself.

The condition of the human immune system weakened by AIDS shares many similarities with a degraded ecosystem like a dying forest. Much has been said about the 'ecological services' that are lost when the forest is destroyed: predictable patterns of rainfall and climate, regularity of stream flow, protection of soils, sustenance of floral and faunal life. As the forest becomes sick and begins to shrink away, the rains come at strange times, summer streams run dry and, in the rainy season, arrive as flash floods, carrying with them tonnes of soil from the hills. Plants and animals that once flourished in specific habitats, depending on particularities of local climate and geography, also start disappearing as those habitats are no more.

Not only is the degraded forest unable to 'perform' the functions that were once part of its nature, it becomes increasingly sensitive to unusual pressure from the outside. Like a human body whose weakened immune system is particularly vulnerable to infection, stresses that were once absorbed by the ecosystem without inflicting significant damage now cause devastation. Such was the case when a massive rainstorm hit the south of Thailand in November 1988.

The south is one of the few regions of Thailand where true rainforest grows. The shape of the land here is reminiscent of the famous Gui Lin in South China, where the mountains seem to shoot straight up from the sea. A century ago, rainforest covered most of the steep limestone mountains and riverine valleys. Today the few patches of rainforest remaining are under threat from dam projects, golf courses, tourism resorts, rubber plantations, illegal logging and encroachment by landless farmers. The process of deforestation in the south is similar to other parts of the country. It began with legal and illegal logging by provincial timber companies. As the trees disappeared, the loggers moved to ever steeper slopes, in spite of complex, though unenforced, regulations that forbade this.

In addition, there was rubber (originally imported to Malaysia from Brazil by the British colonial government), which was found to thrive in the moist, warm climate and well-drained slopes. Local people were provided with rubber trees by government authorities. They were offered special loans and incentives to plant more. Encouraged by the subsidies, some villagers cleared away forest to plant the land with rubber. Others followed the timber companies into the hills, burning away the remaining stumps and planting the tiny saplings in the thin mountain soil.

When an unusually harsh storm hit the southern provinces of Surat Thani and Nakorn Sri Thammarat at the end of November 1988, it was as if the hills simply fell apart. With little cover left on the high slopes, rain went rushing downhill for days on end, causing massive flood damage to villages, towns and farms. As the rain continued, the hills became saturated with water. Unable to withstand the terrible weight, whole mountainsides collapsed, leaving huge gashes of bare rock and red soil exposed. Viewed from the air, the thousands upon thousands of landslides looked like bleeding wounds. Up-rooted trees, branches, rocks, mud, and gravel were transported by the water into the lowlands. These solid rivers, often running several metres high, carried away with them families, houses, whole communities.

The tragedy was unprecedented, but historical records showed that this was not the first storm of such intensity to hit the region. The difference was the level of damage. Many hundreds of people were killed. Communities were devastated, property damages ran into billions of baht. The catastrophe focused public attention as never before on the environmental impacts of logging and deforestation. It catalysed a movement that would result, just a few months later, in the cancellation of commercial logging licenses in the south. The ban was extended throughout the country, and Thailand's logging era was over.

Studies conducted in the aftermath of the storm isolated rubber as a key cause of the devastation, pointing out that the young monoculture planta-tions were unsuited to withstand such heavy rains, which were likely to recur in the future. They recommended an end to state-subsidised rubber plant-ing.[14] Yet more than three years later, the Thai government's Rubber Planta-tion Promotion Fund—financed in part with a loan from the World Bank—continues to encourage southern farmers to expand rubber cultivation. A handful of farmers are trying to keep up forest orchards, where they mix fruit trees with forest species for both market sales and their own consump-tion. But these few face formidable obstacles from the rubber fund which subsidises farmers to plant high-yield rubber saplings, as Muslim elder Lon Madlee from Satun province explained:

They tell us to clear the whole area and plant only one kind of rubber tree. We are not allowed to have mangoes or other fruit trees. If they catch us growing other species, they fine us about 250 baht [USD 10] per tree. They are forcing us to destroy the forest.... It just doesn't make any sense.... I am so angry at this fund.[15]

Numerous other cases of how ecological collapse is affecting communities could be cited here. For example, most of the mangrove forests that once lined both the Gulf of Thailand and Andaman Sea coasts of Thailand's peninsular 'tail' have been cleared away to make way for industrial shrimp farms. This has destroyed the breeding ground of fish and other marine life on which small fishing communities depended. Adding injury to the insult of the 1988 storm, Typhoon Gay hit the provinces slightly north of Surat Thani province exactly one year later, ripping in from the Gulf across the un-protected beaches and wreaking havoc on the land. Again, the damage was astronomical, far worse than the impact of similar typhoons in past years.

In another instance, waste from rock salt mining in northeastern Thailand has turned the water in a nearby river saltier than seawater, shattering the riparian ecosystem and causing desperation among farmers who used the river for gathering vegetables, fishing, watering their buffaloes, drinking and irrigation. Local protest caused the mining to be banned for a few years during the 1980s, and the river appeared to be recovering. But recently, the mining has intensified, in defiance of the ban, and the riverbanks are again shimmering white with the skeletons of fish encrusted in the salty sand.

'Reforestation' schemes (so-called) provide yet another example of how the natural regeneration capacity of ecosystems is being undermined to the detriment of local communities. Large-scale tree plantation projects have been established in land that is deemed to be 'degraded forest', as a way of increasing the country's forest cover. But instead of allowing the forest to regenerate, these lands are cleared of all vegetation and ploughed over several times to create the best growing conditions for fast-growing trees. Not only does this eradicate the remaining floral and faunal diversity (replacing it with non-native monoculture) and erase all chances of natural forest succession, but it also affects local people who may have used those secondary forests for collecting mushrooms, bamboo shoots and other vegetables.

Just as AIDS signals the collapse of human immunity, so environmental degradation undermines the resilience of an ecosystem. The rain no longer falls in its usual cycles, and the soil no longer clings to the hillsides. The streams dry up when once they delivered water to lowland villages throughout the dry season, only to swell to bursting with the coming of the rains. Forests that once provided food and medicine and shelter become waste lands or barren timber factories that can no longer sustain communities. The self-regulating system that functioned according to its own logic as an independent part of the greater whole is suddenly overwhelmed by external forces. The slightest shock, a fire, a typhoon, a common cold—things which would normally cause a minor irritation, but would heal and be quickly forgotten—ravage the weakened system, and sometimes destroy it completely.

The community

When a logging company moved into the northern province of Nan in the late 1980s, local people chased it away with road blocks and large demonstrations. To ensure that the loggers would not return, a Buddhist monk led a ceremony in which huge old trees were 'ordained' with holy saffron monks' robes, and adorned with incense, flowers and candles. Phra Palad Sanguan explained: 'If the forest is all gone, the water will disappear and the people can no longer farm. If they can't farm, all the young people will leave to find work in the cities. And if the community falls apart, there will be nobody to take care of the monks, and the people will lose their beliefs.'[16]

During the 'mobile Cabinet meeting' of 1989 in Chiang Mai, Khru Noi talked about how local people traditionally depended on ecosystems like forests, both physically and spiritually. The forest provided fruit and medicine, shelter and tools. It was also the dwelling place of ancestors' ghosts and guardian spirits. As both providers of life and livelihood and the home of sacred beings, forests were deserving of the highest respect.

As one northern elder explains to her grandchildren, the notions of ecology, spirituality, humility, responsibility and physical human dependence on nature are inseparable:

The forest is the source of the streams we use for farming and drinking water. We preserve the forest so that every year, when we need wood to repair the *muang fai* (traditional irrigation system), there is some place to find it. Every day we need to go into the forest to collect bits of dry wood to use as firewood. We use the forest as grazing grounds for our cows and buffalos and we collect bamboo shoots, mushrooms, fruits and vegetables from the forest to eat. When we're sick we depend on herbal medicines from the forest ... The forest has bestowed kindness on us, and we respect it in return. We make offerings to the sacred spirits of the forests and mountains every year. The spirits of our ancestors, when they die, reside in the forest. So we have to preserve the forest also because it is the residence of people we pay respect to and because it is close to us and part of the villagers' hearts.[17]

Anthropologist Shalardchai Ramitanond of Chiang Mai University says the fundamental premise in the traditional relationship between Thai villagers and their environment is that human beings are but a small part of nature. Highly-developed rules and behaviour have evolved within belief systems about how to treat the spirits that guarded over the precious ecosystems that people depended upon: the hills and valleys, the streams and rivers, the forests and swamps. These formed a way of life based on a vast knowledge of the living natural systems—their management, use and conservation.[18]

There is a growing body of literature on tropical forests describing how cultures living in and around these diverse ecosystems use their environment. Thai forest and lowland farming communities are no exception. The corollary to this dependence, of course, is that as the forests are degraded, villagers have been forced to buy with cash what they once derived from nature. A brief examination of ways people use different ecosystems gives a sense of what in fact is at stake.

Farmers in the northeastern region, for example, derive a significant proportion of their diet from 'natural foods'. Khon Kaen University nutritionist Prapimporn Somnasang has recorded that in rainfed areas of northeast Thailand, villagers gather or hunt more than 100 types of natural foods from their environment, including wild leafy vegetables, roots, shoots and fruits, insects, fish, reptiles and small mammals.[19]

According to Prapimporn, villagers obtain from the forest: vegetables such as sadao, tew, whan, bamboo shoot, sameg, kadon, mong jod, chi paa karjeew flower, narm, hob heb, meid mieng, kee lek, kee khom, kee som, e-roke, care-paa, and whan kee lek; mushroom types such as kradong, ragok kao, din, koa, ploog, pauo, pung, kri, lin mha, na lae, na goa, taan, e-dang; fruits such as makog, makho, mango and manjal; animals such as rat, frog, small toad, ground lizard, snake, rabbit, bird; and insects such as red ant (and its eggs), cicadas, kinum, jilor, tab tow, jiporm, kutgee, kanoon, and mou. She recorded similar abundance of natural foods in streams, ponds and in paddy fields, which she notes, 'produce far more than rice alone'.

Traditionally the collectors of wild foods near to the home, women in the northeast have a complex set of rules governing the gathering of plants. Lisa Leimar-Price notes that these rules are related not only to land tenure (whether legal or customary), but also to taste, market price, abundance or rarity, and even hardiness of the various species. This unwritten regulatory system determines which plants may be collected, during which season, by whom, in what amount, which may be transplanted, which must never be transplanted and so on. They also have complex rules for the conservation of rare plant species.[20]

Just as uses of the natural environment and management techniques vary from ecosystem to ecosystem, so reasons for communities protecting their environment also vary with ecological conditions, local needs and circumstances. A study by the Project for Ecological Recovery compares the different ways local communities in Thailand use forests, and their specific reasons for conserving them.[21] It reports that people in the Muslim fishing village of Dato in Patani province, southern Thailand, have been managing the use of 20 hectares of mangrove forest for more than 150 years. The villagers are fisherfolk who fish in the Bay of Patani, while using wood from the community's forest for making fishing equipment and for fuel. The indirect benefits of protecting the mangroves are, however, more obvious than the direct ones as the coastal forest provides shelter and breeding grounds for marine life that villagers then fish from the bay. Since 1987, people in Dato have been planting trees in an effort to expand the area of mangrove forest.

In contrast, Mien (or Yao) tribal people of Ban Nam Ki in the northern hill evergreen forest of Nan province have for the last three years attempted to formalise a delineation of more than 3,000 hectares of forestland for protection by the community. The ostensible purpose of this decision was conservation of the Matao, a 'sugar palm' fruit tree that only grows in very moist, cool, shaded areas near streams—that is, in intact natural forest. Each Matao tree yields some 30 kilogrammes of fruit per year, providing each Nam Ki family with the equivalent of USD 100 income, annually. On the recommendation of village religious leader, Jua Lin, villagers in 1987 divided up the area among them for control of forest fires and protection against outside encroachers. In addition to Matao, the villagers collect various food and medicinal plants from the forest, as well as timber for house construction, oils and ratan. They also derive drinking water by diverting mountain streams.

Unlike fisherfolk in Dato and forest dwellers in Ban Nam Ki, rice farmers of Chandaiyai in the northeastern province of Yasothorn protect their forest primarily for the mushrooms. There are literally dozens of varieties of mushrooms that grow in specific habitats around different species of old trees, on the forest floor and under the ground. A family can earn between USD 1 and USD 20 per day in local markets, providing an important source of cash income. Survival of the forest also ensures the preservation, for consumption within Chandaiyai, of medicinal herbs, vegetables, mushrooms, fruits, bamboo shoots and so on. Five years ago, in an effort to protect all of these against a government scheme to clear the area for 'reforestation' with eucalyptus trees, local people demarcated more than 1,000 hectares as a community forest.

These are among a growing number of rural communities in Thailand that have been active in protecting their environment. The strategies used and the issues that people emphasise tend to depend on the culture and particularities of the local area. But in many cases, what is at stake is the survival of the whole—the ecosystem, the community and local knowledge. For example, mushrooms usually only grow in dead wood and decaying matter that can be found in the old forests of Chandaiyai. The Matao sugar palm requires the cool, moist, shaded areas that only exist in intact forest. Mushrooms and sugar palm came to represent the natural forest, without which these particular species could not survive. To appreciate the full significance of losing these ecosystems, it is necessary to compare villages such as Chandaiyai and Dato with communities whose forests have been entirely wiped out.

Perhaps the most absolute, and therefore the most violent, destruction of forests that affects local communities is that caused by the big dams. As the river is blocked behind massive concrete structures, the downstream ecosystem is altered by irregular and often polluted water supplies, while the reservoir and much of the surrounding areas are changed beyond recognition. People living in the flood zone are forced to move away—frequently pushing into forest land in the high hills around the new lake—and those below the dam sometimes also find it difficult to stay. Throughout Thailand, communities that once lived in lush lowland valleys have been displaced in this way by dozens of large dams that have been constructed over the last three decades.

A visit to any of the big dam resettlement sites in Thailand makes the links between the integrity of the community and the ecosystem immediately apparent. Communities that once farmed, fished or tended fruit orchards were moved into the high dry land above the reservoir. Typically, compensation payments were used up during the move or shortly after, and, as people were unable to grow food in the arid rocky soils, debts would start to accumulate. The people of Ban Kor, for example, in the northern province of Lampang, were evicted to make way for the country's first hydro dam, the Bhumibhol in 1964. Today they continue to live with none of the running water, irrigation or roads they were promised.

In the resettlement village of a later dam, the Sri Nakharind in Srisawat district of Kanchanaburi province, there are roads, electricity and running water, installed by the Electricity Generating Authority of Thailand (EGAT) as part of the terms of resettlement. But residents can barely afford the utility bills. Because the soil is rocky and dry, it is not possible to grow enough food to eat. They are forced to buy not only rice, vegetables and meat, but sometimes even water because that which is pumped up from the reservoir is often smelly and foul-tasting. Clothes hanging inside refrigerators, purchased in the early years with cash compensation payments, are not a rare sight. These villages are eerie places. They are often treeless and barren, with houses built in grid-like rows. But their most striking feature is the absence of young people.

When asked where his children were, a village elder in Srisawat told us readily which factory his son was working in, but remained vague about his daughters' whereabouts. 'They're working in Bangkok', he said. 'I'm not sure where, they never tell me exactly. But they send money home each month to help pay for food.'[22]

The almost violent reactions of villagers in the northeastern province of Ubon Ratchathani to the Pak Mun hydro dam project also stem from very deep roots, as much connected with the integrity of the environment as with the human community. (Unlike most other hydro dams in Thailand, the Pak Mun will not inundate a large area of forest.) In May 1991, the Thai electricity authority knocked down the small wooden shrine of a local river guardian spirit to make way for construction of the dam. Local people who worshipped the spirit were furious. Hundreds of villagers resurrected a second shrine along the banks of the Mun River and held a two-week-long vigil, which culminated in the occupation of the dam site, forcing the government to review the project. To this day, construction continues, as does the resistance.

When asked why she was opposed to the dam, an elderly woman in Ban Sai Moon village explained in great detail that she feared that fish migrations would be disturbed, and agricultural land and archaelogical sites would be inundated, and then she added: 'We've seen what happened to the people who were moved away from [a nearby] dam. They can't survive on the resettlement land and all their children have moved away. Our life is good here. We just want to keep the community together.'[23]

Khru Noi has described an exodus that has been repeated over and over again in various forms. Whether because of dams or logging, cash-crop cultivation or mining, a combination of environmental destruction, growing consumerism, spiralling debts and the pull of the city has drawn young people towards jobs that can provide the fast income their families need. In this context, the sex trade is an industry that continues to offer high remuneration, especially for women who generally receive lower wages than their male counterparts in the industrial sector.

The vast array of 'products' and 'services' that people gain from a living, healthy forest are the very items that are lost when the ecosystem is degraded, for whatever reason. It can mean a sudden end to cash income, the blocking of irrigation or drinking water supplies, changes in local climate, the devastation of fish stocks, nutritional deficiencies, especially in children, because of the lack of fresh greens and forest fruit, or illness due to the absence of herbal remedies. Or it can imply the destruction of sacred groves or ancestral burial grounds, losses which are far less tangible. What the ecosystem ceases to provide to subsistence communities, the market system must replace. But to buy food, drugs, fertiliser, wood or even water from the market requires cash. And the less able the natural environment to sustain agriculture or produce other saleable items, the more people are forced to look to the commodity that has value on the outside market—the bodies of the young—to obtain badly-needed cash.

The politics

The steady degradation of Thailand's forests and its consequences—one of the most dramatic being the southern floods of 1988—have heightened the sense of urgency about the forest crisis in the public mind. The emergence of AIDS in this same period, and the exponential rate of spread to people of all walks of life, has generated both concern and a demand for solutions. The two situations share similarities at many levels. The physical dimension of deforestation and the accompanying loss of ecological 'services' mirrors the disintegration of human bodily systems as immunity is gradually worn down by AIDS. Environmental erosion and the unravelling of cultures founded on particular ecosystems are among the pressures that force young people to leave their villages and sell their bodies on the market.

The connections, however, extend beyond the physical and cultural. With the sense of urgency about deforestation and AIDS has come a dual political response. On the one hand, there has been a spate of new regulations, laws and policies aimed at stabilising or even reversing these trends. The striking features of these efforts are their direct or implied assigning of blame to the poor, the powerless, the already most disenfranchised members of Thai society; and their tendency to be ineffective or counterproductive. On the other hand, the two crises have provoked an unprecedented swell of civic protest and action that have had considerable impact at the policy level.

Let us first examine existing forestry legislation. The 1964 Forest Reserves Act and the 1985 National Forest Policy are concerned directly with Thailand's forests. The forest reserve law, promulgated while Thailand was still a net timber exporter, provided a mechanism for nationalisation of vast areas of forest land. According to the 1964 act, forests were 'reserved' for logging, and officially brought under the control and ownership of the central government. Concessions would then be meted out to provincial timber companies, which would cut the trees and, in theory, be responsible for re-planting to ensure the forests' regeneration.

Communities already settled in these lands were essentially ignored, as reserves were designated in Bangkok, often without surveys to check the correlation between lines on a map and reality on the ground. The result was that the inhabitants of hundreds of villages became de facto 'illegal forest encroachers': squatters on government land. They became guilty of what Michael Dove calls the 'sin of proximity'—living near degraded resources, they were automatically blamed for the degradation.[24] In the absence of meaningful land reform or an efficient land titling system, it is estimated that today some ten million people—about 25 per cent of the rural population—are living illegally in these state-owned forest reserves. The absurdity of the situation is compounded by the fact that the original purpose of the act, to set aside areas for logging, no longer applies in the post-logging era.

The 1985 forest policy is a product of a different era. Unlike its predecessor which focused on timber extraction, this policy was formulated in an international climate where global forestry and paper industries were searching for empty land in the tropics to replace dwindling supplies of temperate timber. Without openly acknowledging these pressures, the 1985 policy divided Thai forests into two separate spheres: 'commercial forests' and 'conservation forests'. For the former, the policy established guidelines for reforestation, which corresponded perfectly with the needs of these transnational entities. Official forestry department statistics showed that some 29 per cent of the country was under forest cover. Unofficial estimates put the figure at less than 20 per cent. Whatever the real number, there was a general consensus that Thailand was losing something precious. According to the logic of the policy, the forestry department had neither the budget nor the manpower to re-forest the country. (Indeed, during the 96 years since its founding, the department had succeeded in re-planting only about 6,400 square kilometres of trees, an area slightly larger than that which had been deforested each year, on average, over the previous three decades.) The policy therefore proposed that the private sector should be invited to rent land—at a cost of USD 2.50 per hectare per year—inside degraded forest reserves to set up plantations of fast-growing trees. This would in theory generate income through export sales of wood chips and pulp, while turning the balding hills green again. The catch, of course, was the people; ten million of them, who continue to live illegally on these potential plantation sites and are less than anxious to be shunted off land they have inhabited for decades or, in some cases, hundreds of years.

Conservation forest areas, on the other hand, include national parks or wildlife sanctuaries that are managed by foresters for the preservation of wilderness, scenic sites and rare or endangered species. With the exception of tourists and researchers, no people are permitted inside these areas. Villagers are forbidden to hunt or to collect food, wood or medicine.

Meanwhile, existing laws relating to AIDS and the sex industry include the 1960 Prostitution Control Act and the 1980 Communicable Diseases Act.* Given the sheer size of Thailand's sex industry, it remains something of a mystery to many observers that prostitution in Thailand is in fact illegal and is generally viewed as an immoral activity for all concerned. The 1960 act outlawed the sale of sex, specifying fines and sentences for heterosexual and homosexual prostitutes, brothel owners, pimps, owners of establishments who allow prostitution to take place on their premises, and even for 'persons who engage in promiscuous behaviour in brothels'—i.e. clients. And yet prostitution endures, with a vengeance.

For foreign visitors, the most visible form of prostitution is concentrated around major tourist centres. But while these bars and clubs and massage parlours are impossible to miss, they do not constitute the bulk of the Thai sex industry, which serves a local clientele. In addition to the enormous income-generating capacity of the industry, the numbers of people involved, powerful vested interests and the diversity of its forms—from brothels at truck stops and in villages, to cocktail lounges and expensive 'members only' clubs in remote hill resorts—make it virtually impossible to control. During a meeting in 1989, then Minister of Public Health Chuan Leekpai stated plainly that it was understood in the Police Department that prostitutes would not be arrested. Yet it is widely known that sex establishments pay off local police for the 'right' to operate undisturbed in a given area. Occasionally, there are ritualistic raids on sex establishments in which the owner is notified and prepares a number of women for the arrest. They are told what to say, how to behave. They may stay at the local jail for a few hours, or overnight, and are subsequently released and returned to work once the owner has paid the bail.

The prostitution law states that if the officials see fit, prostitutes who have been arrested should be placed in welfare homes where they are to be given moral instruction and job training. Such rehabilitation programmes offer precious little practical assistance to women, cutting off their source of income, teaching them skills like paper flower- or cookie-making that are un-

---

* There are of course other relevant laws and regulations concerning immigration, medical supplies, abortion, drugs, tourism and so on, which are beyond the scope of this article.

likely to provide them with the cash they need, and preaching to them the evil of their ways. Inevitably, it is the poorest women with the least influence or connections who have the misfortune of winding up in these government welfare programmes.

Notably absent from these efforts is the prosecution or punishment of either the clients or owners of sex establishments. In spite of their mention in the prostitution law, it is rare that brothel or bar owners are arrested for their illegal operations. And it is virtually unheard of for clients to be apprehended for engaging in 'promiscuous behaviour'. The sex workers, who are mostly women, are seen to be the immoral party whether they were tricked into the profession by relatives or agents, or entered the industry on their own initiative out of economic necessity. A twisted form of the 'sin of proximity', the blame rests with them, as does the highly selective enforcement of law.

The Communicable Diseases Act, on the other hand, drafted in the pre-AIDS 1970s, was designed to control infectious and potentially fatal diseases such as cholera and tuberculosis. It prescribes a number of heavy-handed measures to control ailments that are transmitted through casual contact. It empowers health officials to cordon off areas where infected people are found. Any person who is suspected of being infected or has come into contact with an infected person must be tested. If found positive, the person must be quarantined without visitors for a length of time deemed appropriate by health officials. If the infected person violates these requirements, he or she is subject to up to six months imprisonment, a fine or both.

With a prostitution act that incriminates sex workers while letting the buyers and agents go free, and an infectious diseases act that prescribes mandatory testing and quarantine, it is hardly surprising that stigmatisation suffered by people with AIDS is intensifying.

Like 'illegal forest encroachers' squeezed by renewed pressure for land from industrial plantation companies and land speculators, sex workers were now guilty not only of illegal and immoral behaviour, but also responsible for the spread of a deadly, contagious disease. These attitudes have carried over into the formulation of new legislation designed, ostensibly at least, to improve these critical situations. But in both cases, laws concerning AIDS and forests are conspicuous in their tendency to criminalise the victims. Instead of examining the whole issue they seem to focus simplistically only on the symptoms. If we don't want people with AIDS in the country, don't give them visas; if prostitutes with AIDS refuse to stop working, lock them up. Similarly, if forests are dying, plant more trees—any species, anywhere. And if people are already living there, arrest them.

As early as 1986, for example, a ministerial regulation issued under the 1979 Immigration Act prohibited aliens with AIDS from entering the kingdom.[25] The public health ministry also officially declared AIDS to be a communicable disease under the 1980 law. But as former Prime Minister Tanin Kraivixien explained in December 1990 to a gathering of international AIDS experts, these measures dealt inadequately with the new disease.*[26] For this reason, he said, new laws and regulations dealing exclusively with Acquired Immune Deficiency Syndrome were needed to cope with the coming epidemic.

One such regulation was a health ministry order that required sex workers to be tested every three months. Those receiving HIV negative results were issued with health certificates, 'green cards', as proof that they were free of AIDS. Those found to be carrying the virus would have their cards withdrawn, and be sent home without any financial compensation. AIDS activist Jon Ungphakorn says this has a devastating effect:

[These are] young women in their prime with high expectations for the future. Suddenly they are informed that they are HIV positive and are sent home with all their dreams crushed, visions of impending death, and the absolute necessity to maintain secrecy about their infection at all times, so as to avoid rejection by their community. It is as though a death sentence has been passed upon them.[27]

The green card policy (the cards are, in fact, pink) opened a Pandora's box of legal confusion and contradiction. If prostitution was illegal, why was the government in the business of issuing safety guarantees that offered protection for male clients? Given that antibodies to the AIDS virus are only detectable months after contraction occurs, were AIDS-free cards not, in any case, a false guarantee? Doctors feared that such a measure would only breed carelessness on the part of sex clients. As Jon Ungphakorn points out, there was no parallel rule requiring men to wear condoms when visiting sex workers.

Blinded by the obsessive focus on sex workers as the source of the virus, many law-makers overlooked the simple fact that most prostitutes (unless they were intravenous drug users) must have picked up AIDS through sex with someone; presumably from a client or a partner. And with more than 15 per cent of young men in parts of the rural north now carrying AIDS, it is clear that poorer prostitutes in those areas who receive five or ten clients a day are at an extremely high risk of picking up the virus. As it turned out, the policy of issuing cards was modified in such a way that cards indicate whether the holder has tested positive to certain sexually transmitted diseases, including HIV, but states clearly that the card should not be used to prove AIDS-free status. Still, brothel-owners sometimes use these health cards as a basis of hiring, or firing, their workers. If the card policy appears to discriminate against women, the draft AIDS law would have been worse.

* Tanin was appointed premier in 1977 by the military junta, which took over the country in October 1976 after a bloody crackdown against pro-democracy student protesters. He is remembered for his ultra-conservative political ideas about the organisation of Thai society.

Former Prime Minister Tanin was the most high-level proponent of the draft AIDS law, which was first proposed at a meeting organised by the Chulabhorn Research Institute in early 1989. Referring to prostitutes, homosexuals, addicts and inmates, he later described its rationale:

Of course, we do not want to discriminate [against] such groups of people, commonly known as 'high risk groups', but how can we reduce such risk from these irresponsible people ... for the general public must also be protected? [Though the new law must] preserve the human rights of AIDS patients and guarantee medical treatment, it should guard against people in these high risk categories who couldn't care less ... whether they will pass on the deadly disease to their sexual partners ... [or] whether ... they themselves may contract the disease.[28]

The draft did offer some conciliatory mention about health care and job protection—doctors were not permitted to refuse patients with AIDS, while employers were forbidden to use AIDS as an excuse to fire employees. But the overwhelming thrust of the draft law criminalised people with AIDS, violated widely-held notions of human rights, and threatened to hasten its spread by forcing people into hiding.

Here are a few examples. Householders would be required to inform authorities if a person living in their house was found to have AIDS. Health officials would be authorised to order 'members of risk groups such as drug addicts, prostitutes, and those who behave in a sexually promiscuous manner' to undertake medical examinations. This also applied to anyone having sex with AIDS-infected persons, children born to women with AIDS, and to prisoners. Such people would be required to inform authorities before leaving their place of residence for more than one month. Finally, health officials would be authorised to order the detention in special welfare homes of persons who refused to comply with these regulations, were deemed likely to abscond, or committed acts causing the spread of infection. They would be held in these 'homes' for up to six months at a time where they would receive job training and moral instruction; concepts that were clearly lifted from the 1960 prostitution law.

One obvious danger of the draft AIDS law was its threat to human rights through mandatory testing, restrictions on travel, confinement to specified areas and detention of people who had committed no crime, and without any judicial procedures. Another problem was its utter non-enforceability. How were authorities to identify persons suspected of sexual promiscuity? Even if we assume the lower estimate of 100,000 sex workers in Thailand, surely there are at least a few times more clients than this. Would they not all constitute 'suspected AIDS carriers', in the words of the draft, by virtue of their contact with prostitutes? These two dangers combined to make the draft AIDS law unenforceable and ineffective at best, and at worst, a potential tool of political repression that could, if it fell into the wrong hands, be selectively applied to persons deemed undesirable by the powers-that-be.

The draft almost immediately sparked an uproar among doctors, social scientists and activists working on issues ranging from women's, children's and gay rights, to prostitution, public health and rural development. Pressure to alter fundamentally the draft was so great that, in November 1989, a public hearing was held. It became the first event of its kind for consideration of a piece of draft legislation. Lawyers on the drafting committee stood their ground, insisting that it would be unrealistic to legislate for men to wear condoms with prostitutes, and that the 'public good' must override idealistic human rights concerns. They were answered by two basic criticisms: (1) Draconian measures do not stop AIDS because, unlike cholera which is transmitted by casual contact, this virus spreads in limited ways and lies dormant for several months, making it impossible to identify carriers. As politically attractive as they may appear, forced testing and incarceration have no public health basis; (2) if passed, such a law would increase stigmatisation of people with AIDS, push them underground, out of the reach of medical care, and possibly accelerate the spread of the epidemic. In October 1991, the draft was finally axed during a brief, but historic meeting at Government House.

The Thai government's response to the forest crisis has followed a similar pattern, reinforcing misconceptions and intensifying social and ecological disruption. Communities living illegally in state forest reserve land are trapped in a messy legal tangle, faced with the unpredictable attitude of responsible authorities who may be grudgingly tolerant one week, and decide to enforce land and forest laws the next. Communities who want to plant trees to accelerate natural forest regeneration are discouraged by their lack of security on the land. People in villages such as Huay Kaew, Dato and Nam Ki are not only discouraged from their efforts to protect the forest— they have been penalised and persecuted. Meanwhile, companies looking to set up plantations (the favoured species is eucalyptus camaldulensis) have found it necessary either to bribe villagers off the land, or rely on the police or military's more persuasive tactics. But government officials clearly cannot arrest all these illegal encroachers. As village land rights advocates have pointed out, there are not enough jails in the country. Yet the existing laws make it easier to get rid of individuals or whole communities in areas where the land is needed for other purposes, or simply to teach surrounding villages a 'lesson'.

As corporations employ different strategies to get hold of large tracts of land for plantations, villagers have been squeezed from different directions. In some areas, good forest was cleared to make it appear 'degraded', only to be replaced by monoculture tree farms. In others, eucalyptus plantations are believed to have affected the water table and the productivity of crops in adjacent fields. Villagers have been offered bribes, forced to sell their (unofficial) rights by speculators, or simply evicted from their homes by armed men. When foresters planted saplings in rice and crop fields in Buriram province, farmers became so angry that they burnt down a government eucalyptus nursery. Where they have moved onto land near commercial tree farms, villagers saw their lives changed beyond recognition.

Sanitsuda Ekachai writes of the experiences of Chand Poonsawad, a farmer and mother of nine in Chachoengsao province, heart of Thailand's eucalyptus country. Chand explained that she and her husband sold their land to pay off farm debts incurred eight years ago due to falling crop prices:

Since the plantations, the land has just dried up and the rice crops have failed. It was never like this. Water for the paddy fields must be pumped up from the canal, which becomes drier every year. But when the annual flood comes, water does not go away as quickly as before. The dykes around the plantations keep the fields flooded, destroying our rice crops. Things get worse and worse. I don't know what to do. I can't eat. I can't sleep. There's never a meal I eat till I'm full. I'm a rice farmer, but now I have to buy rice to eat. It's painful. I think and think. That's why I'm a wreck.[29]

In the midst of numerous, sometimes violent, confrontations between communities and state agencies allied with transnational corporations, a draft law was proposed that would make it even easier to set up these industrial plantations. The draft Plantation Act followed the spirit of the 1985 forest policy, eliminating bureaucratic hassles that inconvenience companies. But it failed to acknowledge land tenure issues, or the plight of people who live in areas that Bangkok authorities have set aside for tree farms. It also ignored preliminary evidence that single-species eucalyptus plantations cause negative ecological impacts, and are only profitable for large companies.[30] As the barrage of critics against the 1985 forest policy repeated time and again, this draft law—like the policy on which it was based—equated tree farms with natural tropical forests. Using a definition of 'degraded' forest based on the amount of harvestable timber, the draft law effectively encouraged companies to clear away secondary forest and replace it with monocultures.

Though the Plantation Law was eventually passed, the 'guts' were removed from it due to sustained lobbying by critics of forest policy. As it stands now, the law promotes only tree plantations of indigenous species—not eucalyptus, and remains highly unsatisfactory to the transnational corporations that lobbied for its promulgation.

The networks of social resistance that have emerged in response to top-down laws and policies ostensibly designed to cope with AIDS and deforestation have had similar kinds of impact. The setbacks that these movements have experienced are less surprising, under the circumstances, than the gains.

After years of public pressure and debate, some of the most potentially dangerous AIDS legislation has been removed or weakened. Indeed, there exist today in Thailand anonymous blood testing centres, anonymous clinics and counselling services, and an explicit state policy against mandatory testing. As part of the seventh national development plan (1992–1996), no doctor may refuse to treat a person with AIDS, and it is forbidden to screen patients or potential employees for the virus. Blood donors are, as a rule, not informed of their sero-positive status unless they request to know. While these are some of the measures AIDS activists have fought hard for, they insist that enforcement remains difficult and stigmatisation does still occur. Nevertheless, when compared with the state-sanctioned discrimination that persists in many neighbouring countries, or with what it would mean for Thai AIDS patients if some of the more draconian measures had been implemented, the significance of these achievements becomes immediately apparent.

It is possible to trace similar dynamics within Thai forest politics. The Thai community forest movement that emerged in the mid-1980s and continues to gain momentum today is not just a fight for rights over the forest. It is also a fight for cultural survival. Farming communities confront formidable opponents, from government foresters and local police to army officers and transnational corporations. These forces would expropriate their common woods and agricultural land for more 'productive' purposes, effectively pushing villagers farther into natural forest or into the industrial labour force. And yet, despite these relentless trends, Thailand became the first country in Asia to legislate a full-scale logging ban in 1989. Plans for massive expansion of monoculture tree farms have been thwarted by a moratorium since 1990 on private plantations in government land, and the 1991 plantation act was essentially castrated as a result of continued pressure from the ground. At the same time, a draft community forestry bill has been drawn up, which would, if passed—for the first time in a century—give legal basis for communities to control, manage and use natural forests for their local needs.

The virgin/forest

The public support that has allowed community movements to grow strong goes beyond an abstract sense of justice. It reflects a growing realisation that the intellectual separation of forests into 'conservation' and 'economic' zones simply does not work; that political dispossession is not only unjust, it is also ecologically unviable. Over the past nine decades since the creation of the forestry department, foresters have failed in their task of protecting forests from the people and for the state. If selective logging and sustained yield management had worked, the forests would be here today to prove it.

They are not. And in the post-logging era, handing over vast tracts of sec-ondary or degraded forest to companies to be made over as mono-culture tree stands, moves even farther away from the diverse ecological benefits of the natural forest.

As communities have resisted, we have learned that what is degraded land in the eyes of a forester may be a valuable resource for villagers; not perhaps for the timber, but for a myriad of other things. Their struggles have forced us to confront questions that no government has yet seriously answered. Where will people go if half the forest is preserved for animals while the other half is given over to companies? Where does human society belong if forests are split between 'normalised', uniform tree farms on one side, and pristine, untouched wilderness on the other? A bleak biological wasteland, manipulated and commoditised for industrial production at one extreme, pitted against virgin nature abounding with non-human life, protected by barbed wire from the destructive hand of man. Total abstention on one side of the fence, and violent rape on the other.

Just as farmers' struggles have gone beyond mere fights for abstract justice, the demands of the Thai women's movement for equal rights may be eclipsed by the more urgent task of staying alive. In the early days of AIDS, everyone's attention was focused on the so-called 'high risk groups'. As the epidemic progresses, it becomes clear that there exists another 'group' (if they can even be called that), who are extremely vulnerable due to their fre-quent exposure to AIDS, and their virtual inability to protect themselves. These are of course the women, the wives, the female partners of men who frequent prostitutes. National surveys show that between December 1990 and June 1991, the number of pregnant women infected with AIDS jumped from 0.3 per cent to 0.7 per cent.[31] As of the time of writing, at least one in 100 women giving birth in hospitals or clinics are carrying the AIDS virus. And rates of infection among pregnant women are many times higher in some provinces.

The 'respectable woman' (kulasatri) and the whore have become intimately connected by a virus that is transmitted through sexual contact. What is a woman to do? What advice have women's rights activists to give their sisters who, through no apparent fault of their own, find themselves being infected with a fatal disease by their very own husbands. What does a mother tell her daughter about love and survival in the age of AIDS?

Prior to AIDS, prostitution concerned two parties only: the buyers and the purveyors of sex. 'Respectable women' did not enter the discussion, except to cast moral aspersions on their unruly husbands and their erstwhile bed-mates. And not only unenlightened fellows—such as lawyers drafting the AIDS law who said: 'If we stop all prostitution, this would encourage nega-tive sexual behaviour ... therefore, we must just accept it'—view the sex in-dustry as an evil necessity. The Thai woman has also internalised this myth:

preferring that before marriage her boyfriend sleep with a prostitute to protect her own virginity; upholding a one-sided monogamy, while her husband has relations with commercial sex workers; and reinforcing the curious idea that a man's sexual needs are stronger and more important than hers.

As nature has been divided into two distinct conceptual spheres, so woman is herself divided. As a respectable woman she despises her morally inferior sister, and yet she is taught to believe she 'needs' the prostitute to protect her virginity and to absorb her man's 'negative sexual behaviour'. Her view of the prostitute oscillates between scorn and pity. Either the sex worker is a poor helpless child, tricked into a life of sin, or she is easy and weak-willed, an essentially immoral being from whom the respectable woman should keep a healthy distance. The AIDS epidemic has closed this distance. Respectable womanhood has finally been dragged into the centre of this discussion, as the Thai woman is forced to confront her sexuality head on.

The naïveté, borne of being isolated from one's sexuality, was once a woman's greatest asset. In the age of AIDS, it is a fatal liability. It is not enough to counsel couples to use condoms, to beseech men to be more careful, or stop frequenting prostitutes entirely. Health ministry posters that portray the pregnant woman infected with AIDS worrying about the future of her unborn child may be an accurate depiction, but they do not offer particularly useful advice on what a woman should do to protect herself. Is she to isolate herself from her husband? Is she to have sex with him only on condition that he use a condom with her? And what if he refuses? What if she is not accustomed to making such demands in the first place? It is clear that a Thai woman in the age of AIDS—especially a young woman—must know her body well and understand her sexuality before she can be expected to discuss it with her future partner. But who will teach her? Who will break the deadly silence of modesty?

AIDS requires women to make conscious, active decisions about the most intimate areas of our lives. As women we can no longer afford to deny our sexual selves, to continue defining ourselves in terms of men's relationship to us, and to view prostitution as an industry we need for protection. Nor can we afford to turn our backs on it because it has entered right into our lives. As the engine that drives this epidemic, the sex industry must be confronted by all women and men. But confronting the underpinnings of prostitution will also rattle the foundations of respectable womanhood; it will force us to question our passivity, our forced virginity, our repression of sexuality. Facing ourselves may expose the simple truth that the wall separating the virgin and the whore—so deeply internalised by women—never really offered any protection. Indeed, perhaps its only true function was the reinforcement of male domination.

It will be neither easy nor painless to move beyond the separation. We jealously guard the innocence of the young girl while her sisters sell their bodies to keep the family's land. We covet islands of diversity, but close our eyes to the ecological devastation surrounding them. The fear of devaluing virginity is as wrenching as our apprehensions about the survival of the last 'hot spots' of 'virgin' forest land. This absolute dichotomy, which forms the conceptual basis of natural resource and development policies, denies local people's history and knowledge. It ignores generations and centuries of cultures that have learned how to preserve and enhance diversity because they depended upon it. The same division internalised by women robs us of our own stories, our own self-knowledge.

Against the insidious trend of ecological collapse, a life force is expressed in a multiplicity of forms through people's movements. It can be found in the words of Lon Madlee, the Muslim elder who imitates the structure of the forest by mixing different species with his rubber trees to maintain biodiversity, save himself from debt and keep his family together. Or in the direct opposition to laws and policies that would further erode biological diversity in favour of more 'efficient' systems of production. The same life force was there in the fierce protest against the draft AIDS law, that would have criminalised the very people who are most in need of compassion. And it can be seen in the actions of forest monks in all parts of Thailand, who have 'ordained' huge old trees with holy saffron robes.

On the ecological front, the battles of farmers and forest people to remain on their land and to have their stories heard are breaking down this dichotomy. The community forest, where local people have power and responsibility over local resources, is the thin end of a wedge, forcing itself between these mutually exclusive views of nature. Neither is it pristine, nor barren. But by providing security for communities, it greatly improves the chances for survival of un-peopled areas of biodiversity. Is it possible that these people's movements, that seek to make peace with the Earth, hold some inspiration for women? As they ease the tensions between two natures, can we also bridge the schism that separates ourselves?

In the intensity of a crisis there is a tendency to move towards greater polarisation, to stigmatise and ostracise and separate. This crisis of ecological collapse demands that to survive, we move instead towards healing, towards the whole. As women, we must learn to become the measure of ourselves, in body and in mind. We must find a strength within that is so deep and so rooted that it cannot be undermined.

Where production and preservation have been sharply divided, plant diversity must return to the fields, gathering must be permitted in the sacred forest, human beings must re-discover their small place in nature. This is not to say that single communities hold global solutions. Nor is it the case that a single individual can speak for her sex. Rather, by unlocking the gate between two opposing natures we will liberate human knowledge and creativity, which is after all where the hope for ecological recovery lies.

Notes

1. Viravaidhya, M., Obremskey, S. A., and Myers, C., *The Economic Impact of Aids on Thailand*, The Population and Community Development Association, Bangkok, 1991.
2. The four large hydro-electric or irrigation dam projects that have been cancelled or put on hold as a result of popular resistance since 1987 are Nam Choan in Kanchanaburi province, Kaeng Sua Ten in Phrae province, Kaeng Krung in Surat Thani province and Haew Narok in Nakhon Nayok province. The only dam project that has gone ahead is the Pak Mool in Ubon Ratchathani. It is currently under construction despite continued opposition from local people.
3. Oranong Phaowattana has since been ousted from her position as village headwoman, reportedly because of resentment from her male colleagues.
4. Sapphasit Khumpraphan insists that the 800,000 figure is based on a province-by-province survey of brothels and other sex establishments.
5. Letter to the editor of the *Bangkok Post* by Mechai Viravaidhya, 1991.
6. Ibid.
7. Ungphakorn, J., 'The Political and Humanitarian Requisites for Effective AIDS Policies', (unpublished paper), Bangkok, 1989.
8. Statistics for 1988 of the Epidemiology Department, Ministry of Public Health, Bangkok.
9. Interview with Dr Vicharn Vithayasai in December 1989. These figures have since been quoted extensively both in Thailand and in the Western media.
10. Nopkesorn, T., Sungkarom, S., and Sornlum, R., 'HIV Prevalence and Sexual Behaviours among Thai Men Aged 21 in Northern Thailand', Kai Somdej Pranaresuan Hospital, Third Army, Phitsanuloke, 1991.
11. Interview with Dr Vicharn Vithayasai, see note 9.
12. Statistics for June 1991 of the Epidemiology Department, Ministry of Public Health, Bangkok.
13. See Viravaidhya, M., et al., op. cit.
14. *Safeguarding the Future: Restoration and Sustainable Development in the South of Thailand*, National Economic and Social Development Board and United States Agency for International Development, Bangkok, 1989.
15. Muslim elder Lon Madlee spoke at the People's Forum, a parallel conference during the October 1991 General Annual Meeting of the World Bank in Bangkok.
16. Phra Palad Sanguan was among several forest monks speaking at a conference on hilltribe knowledge of ecology, organised by the Mountain People's Centre for Development and Education, Chaing Mai, 1991.
17. Cited in Permpongsacharoen, Witoon, 'Tropical forest movements: Some lessons from Thailand' in a volume on tropical forests (in German), Arbeit Gemeinschaft Regenwald, 1991, p. 2.
18. Interview with Shalardchai Ramitanond in June 1991.
19. Prapimporn, S., Rathakette, P., and Rathanapanya, S., 'The Role of Natural Foods in Northeast Thailand' in *Rapid Rural Appraisal in Northeast Thailand*, edited by Lovelace, G. W., Subhadhira, S., and Simaraks, S., Khon Kaen, 1988.

20. From a paper by Lisa Leimar-Price at the Annual Conference of the Northwest Regional Consortium for Southeast Asian Studies, Oregon, November 1991, and personal communication.
21. Project for 'Ecological Recovery, People and the Future of Thailand's Forests: An Evaluation of the State of Thailand's Forests Two Years After the Logging Ban', Bangkok, 1991.
22. Conversations with villagers in the Sri Nakharind Dam Resettlement Site, February 1988. They were among the many different groups of people in Kanchanaburi province who opposed construction of the Nam Choan Dam.
23. Interviews with people living along the banks of the Mun River in and near the flood zone of the Pak Mun Dam, Ubon Ratchanthani province, 1990.
24. From Michael Dove's keynote speech to the 1991 Annual Conference of the Northwest Regional Consortium for Southeast Asian Studies.
25. Ministerial Regulation Number 11, 1986 issued under the Immigration Act, 1979, which prohibits aliens with AIDS from entering the Kingdom. Cited in a speech by H. E. Tanin Kraivixien to the Chulabhorn Research Institute's International Congress on AIDS, Bangkok, 1990.
26. Ibid.
27. Ungphakorn, J., op. cit.
28. Speech by H.E. Tanin Kraivixien, see note 25.
29. Ekachai, Sanitsuda, 'A life broken by plantations', *Bangkok Post*, February 27, 1991. See also her book, *Behind the Smile*, TDSC, Bangkok, 1990.
30. In addition to similar complaints by villagers from several regions of Thailand— and indeed, from countries as far-flung as India, Portugal and Brazil—there are a number of scientific studies that indicate potential for negative ecological impacts of large-scale eucalyptus plantations. See Homchand, C., Mongkholsawad, S., and Tulaphitak, T., 'Impact of Eucalyptus Plantation on Soil Properties and Subsequent Cropping', United States Agency for International Development, Bangkok, 1989; Petmak, P., Kietvuttinon, B., and Boontawee, B., 'Some Ecological Impacts of Planting Eucalyptus', Silvicultural Research Subdivision, Royal Forestry Department, Bangkok, 1986; Craig, I., Wasunan, S., and Saenlao, M., 'Effects of Paddy-Bund-Planted Eucalyptus Trees on the Performance of Field Crops', paper presented at the Fifth Annual Farming Systems Conference, Kamphaengsaen, 1988; Jirasuktaveekul, W., and Witthawatchutikul, P., 'Soil Moisture of Eucalyptus Plantation and Abandoned Area at Ban Huay Ma Fuang, Rayong', Research Section, Watershed Management Division, Royal Forest Department, Bangkok, 1988.
31. Statistics for June 1991, Epidemiology Department, Ministry of Public Health, Bangkok.

Killing Legally with Toxic Waste
Women and the Environment in the United States

Penny Newman

Introduction

It has been twenty years since Earth Day placed ecological issues on the public policy table in the United States for the first time. It has been twenty years since the Stockholm Environment Conference put forth the threats to our planet in an international forum. And yet in those twenty years the situation of our planet's health and well-being has worsened, not improved. Those receiving the brunt of this increased poisoning are the women and children living either in the poor, rural areas or in urban ghettos and barrios. The chemical pollution of the twentieth century is affecting their health in a permanent and devastating way.

The cooperative approach to negotiating changes in order to control pollution has not worked. For those of us living in polluted communities, expecting the polluters to be 'good corporate citizens' has proven deadly. Relying on our governmental system for protection through laws and regulations has left our communities vulnerable. And the established environmental movement has simply disregarded the concerns of the poor, outlining an agenda that is devoid of their input and blind to their plight. But there is hope.

Led almost exclusively by women, a new social justice movement has arisen in the United States to confront environmental hazards. The Movement for Environmental Justice comprised of the people who have suffered most— the women and children, the poor and people of colour—are stepping forward to demand a change. These women, often ridiculed as 'hysterical housewives', recognise that environmental hazards are health hazards, and those hazards are killing children and others in our communities. It is no longer a question of how much pollution is acceptable; the demand is that there be no more pollution. The battle is for survival.

These women have refused to play the game by the rules of the old environmental movement and have been the ones to insist that enough is enough. The 'environment' for the women in our communities is the place in which we live, and that means everything that affects our lives. The agenda must reflect that. For someone having to drink polluted water, ozone depletion is not an issue which ranks high on her list of concerns. For mothers of children dying from cancer, global warming is a non-issue.

Personal experiences

The impact of toxic chemicals came to the forefront of our nation with the 1978-1980 struggle at Love Canal where 900 families fought for and won relocation after they had discovered that their neighbourhood was built next to 21,000 tons of toxic wastes. As our nation watched Lois Gibbs and her neighbours literally fight for their lives, other women also began looking around their own communities.

During this time my community was discovering the Stringfellow Acid Pits. Like most women involved in these battles, we woke up one day to discover that our families were being damaged by toxic contamination, a situation over which we had little, if any, control. It was not an issue in which we chose to become involved, rather we did it because it was a matter of our own survival.

The Stringfellow Acid Pits were a permitted hazardous waste disposal site licensed by the State of California in 1955 to accept deadly wastes from corporations throughout California. Elevated in a boxed canyon above the small rural community of Glen Avon in southern California, the pits accepted more than 34 million gallons of liquid wastes including heavy metals (lead, cadmium, chromium, arsenic); organic solvents, (trichlorethylene—TCE, tetrachloroethylene—PCE, chlorinate, diphenyls—PCBs, and chloroform); pesticides (including DDT); and large amounts of sulphuric, nitric and hydrochloric acids (hence its nickname).

It was not until 1978 that the 'acid pits' came to my attention. Until that time I had led a fairly normal life, teaching a special education class, raising two sons, and living a typical middle class American life. But in 1978, southern California—a normally dry, arid area—experienced very heavy rains, and that was when it all began for me.

As the rains continued, the site, which was a series of open pits, ponds and lagoons, began to overflow. The dam that was supposed to hold back the millions of gallons of toxic chemicals began to fall apart. In order to relieve some of the pressure against the dam, a governmental agency decided to release 1 million gallons of toxic chemicals into our community. The chemicals were pumped out of the ponds and into Pyrite Creek, a little dirt wash that runs down the canyon alongside the road and into Glen Avon.

Over a five day period, chemicals were released from the site to flow through our community—over public roads, flooding our homes, and inundating the elementary school just three-quarters of a mile below the site. During that entire time we were not informed of what was occurring; we assumed that the puddles our children played in and the water our animals stood in was just rain water runoff. We had no idea that we were being exposed to toxic chemicals and it was not until people noticed children's tennis shoes falling apart, and Levis disintegrating that we began to suspect something.

Our community stepped forward to demand that the exposure to chemicals stop, and that the site be cleaned up. And we have won! We are no longer exposed to the chemicals at Stringfellow, we no longer drink contaminated water and we no longer rely on others to protect us. We are empowered, taking full responsibility for our lives and demanding a say in what happens at the site.

Because of that flooding episode and the hundreds that we did not know about between 1955 and 1978, there has been a dramatic and permanent impact on our community's health. My own family exemplifies some of the health problems we continue to see in the community. When I moved into Glen Avon in 1966, I was 19, newly married, three months pregnant with my first child, and very excited at starting a new life in a new home in a small rural community. Just the kind of place I dreamed of raising my children. Five-and-a-half months into the pregnancy I miscarried.

The next year I gave birth to a son, Eric, born six-weeks premature and barely weighing five pounds. Eric had health problems from the beginning. He suffered from allergic reactions to everything and experienced asthma attacks. My husband and I would take turns lying awake at night listening to him breathe, knowing that at some point we would have to rush him to the hospital. If we took him too soon they would just send us home but if we waited too long it became life-threatening.

Eric also had a congenital hip defect that required him being in braces for the first five years. He has vision in only one eye and is classified as legally blind in the other. At the age of five when he started attending the elementary school, he began having severe abdominal pains. After a year of testing to identify the problem he was rushed to hospital in the middle of the night and emergency surgery was performed for what was believed to be appendicitis. Instead Eric had his gall bladder removed—an extremely unusual condition for a five year old.

My younger son, Shawn, was born in Glen Avon, too. He seemed to be healthier; that is, until he began attending the school. Shawn started to suffer from a problem that made his skin look like a dry river bottom; it cracked open and oozed, making him vulnerable to infections. He also developed asthma. In 1978 when the school was inundated with chemical flood waters, Shawn was one of the children playing in the puddles. Shortly thereafter, he began experiencing double vision, sometimes describing how he could see two baseball bats or how basketball poles were standing on top of each other. He then began having dizzy spells, to the point of being nauseated and I would have to hold him to convince him he was not moving. And then the headaches began. Shawn would scream from the pain, begging me to stop it hurting, but none of the medicines prescribed stopped the pain.

Even big, burly men did not escape the wrath of Stringfellow. My husband developed an allergic reaction to almost everything. He would get hives, big, red welts all over his body, which the government always dismissed as skin rashes. But they had a big impact on our lives. Such welts not only showed up on his arms and legs but also in his throat, closing off his air passage, and making it difficult to breathe. We'had a plastic tube next to our bed so that if his throat swelled shut, I could insert the tube allowing him to breathe once again.

When we first started working on Stringfellow we thought that once the exposures to the chemicals stopped, our health problems would disappear and our lives would once again normalise. We now realise that it is not that easy. The chemicals have a dramatic, permanent effect on all body systems, so that although many symptoms improve, damage is still there. We are finding that the immune systems of many of us have been damaged to the point where our bodies simply cannot respond, making us vulnerable to illness. And the threat of what may lie in the future looms over us. Of the 21 people on the staff at the elementary school in 1978, 17 have either died or have severe, unusual diseases. This past year alone, five teachers have died of cancer. The chance of developing cancer in the future is there for all of us and the future of our children is in great question. In one testing session where four young men between the ages of 18 and 21 underwent fertility tests, three were shown to be sterile. The problems the corporations and the state have created not only threaten us now but future generations as well. Can our children have children? Will their children be 'normal'?

Winning! A new approach

With experiences similar to mine occurring throughout the country it has been women who have stepped forward to demand action. The mothers in America *know* when something is wrong. They *know* when their children are ill. Women, rooted in the community, know when things are not right. And it has been these women who have forced change.

For Cathy Hinds in East Gray, Maine, the knowledge that spurred her to action was the loss of feeling in her extremities, asthma attacks and finally the death of her newborn son. For Patricia Nonnon in Bronx, New York, it was the death of her daughter Kerri, from chemical exposure to the Pelham Bay landfill. For Guadalupe Nuno it was finding in her home high levels of lead that threatened her children. And for Lois Gibbs at Love Canal, New York, it was the realisation that chemicals from Hooker Chemical Company caused her five-year old son, Michael, to be hospitalised and placed under an oxygen tent because of pneumonia; and inflicted her daughter, Missy, with a rare blood disease.

Neither the polluters, the system nor the environmental movement were of any help at Love Canal or at any of the other dump sites around the country. What *was* helpful was the loose network of women at the various sites who in reading about each other's battles in newspapers and seeing news accounts on television began contacting each other for information, encouragement and resources. The need to formalise that network led Lois Gibbs and other 'veterans' of the Love Canal toxic disaster to form the Citizens' Clearinghouse for Hazardous Wastes (CCHW) in 1981. They wanted CCHW to be the kind of organisation that would have been helpful when they were fighting for their children. This is why the motto for CCHW is, *'helping people to help themselves'*. Our goal is not only to stop pollution, but to do it in such a way that people, primarily women, can take control of their own lives.

For the last ten years, CCHW has been a support mechanism encouraging and assisting the thousands of grassroots groups around the country. Within that network, communities are taking on some of the most powerful forces in the country, including the petrochemical industry, landfill operators, incinerator companies, government bureaucracies, and other pollution and waste-related entities intertwined in the problem. We are not advocates for grassroots groups, they can speak for themselves; we will not do anything for people that they can do for themselves, for that creates dependency; and we will not intervene in a situation unless we are asked to by local folks for they are the ones who must decide on the agenda and ultimately fight the battle. Our strong conviction is that public policy can, and should, be changed from the bottom up and CCHW is designed to be a resource for groups doing that. But, perhaps, we should now consider the nature of what we are up against.

The problem

According to the US Environmental Protection Agency (EPA) an estimated 275 million metric tons of hazardous waste are disposed of each year. That is about 2,500 pounds for every woman, man and child in the nation.

The chemical industry in the United States expanded its use and production of synthetic organic chemicals from 1 million tons in 1940 to over 125 million tons in 1987—a 12,500 per cent increase. The use of these and other chemicals creates numerous toxic hazards, from transportation spills and accidental releases to leaking storage tanks and indoor air contamination.[1] In 1989, the US manufacturing facilities released over 18 billion pounds of toxic chemicals directly into either air, water, land or underground wells.[2]

The waste produced from these facilities creates yet another health hazard for the American people in the form of toxic dumps and polluted communities. The list of contaminated sites acknowledged by the US Environmental Protection Agency (EPA) continues to grow. The EPA's National Priorities List (NPL) of the worst sites in the nation numbers over a thousand, with another 31,552 sites waiting for inclusion. The Congressional Office of Technology Assessment (OTA) believes the NPL list will reach over 10,000 sites during the 1990s and that the list of sites that should be considered for inclusion is somewhere between four and 10 times greater than the number acknowledged.[3]

The problems associated with toxic chemicals in the United States are not confined to our borders. The US and other industrialised countries are generously sharing the problem by exporting poisons to Third World countries. According to one recent study, millions of pounds of banned, unregistered and restricted pesticides are exported from the US every year. United States Customs records, obtained by the Foundation for Advancements in Science and Education (FASE), indicate that between March and May of 1990 pesticides which are suspected to cause cancer, mutagenesis and adverse reproductive effects were exported at a rate of at least three tons each hour. Sri Lanka received over 1,000,000 pounds of pesticides in that three-month period, with India, Thailand and Indonesia receiving between 100,000 and 200,000 pounds each.[4]

Toxic compounds are detectable in the body tissue of most, if not all, Americans. Recent tests by EPA's National Human Adipose Survey show that most likely all Americans have toxic compounds stored in their fatty tissues; 100 per cent of people's tissue samples in one recent test contained styrene, xylene isomers, 1,4-dichlorobenzene and ethylphenol. Some of these chemicals are known or suspected to cause cancer, birth defects and other health problems.[5]

Industry's role

Is it that the corporations just do not understand the impact of their poisons on people? One wonders if they simply do not know what they are doing. Or if they simply do not care. Can greed and the desire to maximise profits simply override concern about the damage to people and the environment? Internal memoranda from two corporations give us a glimpse into the decision-making process and the mentality of some managers of big business.

An internal memo from Occidental Petroleum Corporation outlines the attitude on the continued manufacturing of DBCP, a substance known to cause sterility and cancer in workers. The memo reads, in part:

This [a method for evaluating the future potential liability] becomes especially important in a case such as DBCP where known health effects have been observed....
1. Estimate the maximum number of people in-house who would be exposed to

DBCP during the course of manufacture.... 2. Estimate the maximum number of people who might be exposed to DBCP in transportation, distribution and use.... 3. Determine the normal temporary or permanent sterility rate in the general population. Also the normal cancer rate.... 4. Assume that 50 per cent of the normal rate for those people exposed may file claims of effects ... for sterility and cancer.... 5. Calculate the potential liability including 50 per cent for legal fees.... Should this product still show an adequate profit, meeting corporate investment criteria, the project should be considered further.[6]

At another company, in a two-page handwritten note, a Gulf Resources and Chemical Corporation vice president in Idaho outlined estimates of how much Gulf would have to pay if it continued to expose children in the town of Kellogg to lead-contaminated smoke. The note's calculations were based on a 1970 lead-poisoning incident at an Asarco Inc. smelter in El Paso, Texas. The note begins, 'El Paso—200 children—USD 5 to USD 10,000 per kid' and is followed by a reference to the Gulf operation indicating an estimated liability for poisoning 500 Kellogg children at 'USD 6-7 million'. Even knowing the damage it was doing to the children of the area, Gulf *increased* the emissions from the smelter to cash in on the high lead prices of 1974. The children of Kellogg suffered the consequences. According to an EPA Inspector General's report, '... the blood-lead levels were the highest ever recorded. Of the 179 children living within one mile of the smelter, 99 per cent had a blood-lead level of over 40 µg/dl. (The current standard is 10 µg/dl). The highest level recorded is 164 µg/dl; 41 children had a blood-lead level over 80, the level established for lead poisoning.'[7]

The system's role

In many ways our system condones the deadly, sometimes deliberate acts these corporations perpetrate against our own people. As Lin Nelson writes in *The Place of Women in Polluted Places*, '...the bleak, sometimes horrific, conditions that oppress us are created not only by the polluters, but also by the architects of policy, science, and health care who at best patch things up with distracting, ineffective, and sometimes dangerous "solutions".'[8] We have slowly, steadily, allowed the polluters, even when they are repeat offenders, to become respectable as they buy their way into our public policy decisions.

Our government and industry have become accomplices working against the interest of poor communities. The laws simply do not protect people. How else can we explain the statistics? How else can we explain the fact that we now have a system where *it is perfectly legal to kill people with toxic chemicals?!*

When we allow discussions about an 'acceptable risk' of one in 1,000 or one in 10,000 we are accepting that it is all right to kill one person in every 1,000 or 10,000. We have allowed the premise that it is all right for someone to die so that a facility can operate. These calculations are made for each individual chemical under perfect operating conditions. No calculations are made for the effects of people being exposed to two or more chemicals simultaneously, and of course the 'kill rate' increases during accidents or 'illegal' discharges. The law permits corporations to kill as long as they stay within set limits.

In devising these standards, women and children are not considered. The calculations are based on occupational exposures for healthy males working an eight-hour day, five days a week, wearing safety equipment in controlled settings. But the most vulnerable populations of our communities, children, pregnant women and the elderly, are often exposed for 24 hours a day, seven days a week with no protective clothing. These populations apparently do not even warrant consideration when industry is determining what the 'acceptable risk' will be.

Ultimately, we rationalise it all. We make the danger antiseptic by speaking in terms of standards, risk assessments, and statistics. We never put a face on that one person in 10,000. We allow ourselves to believe that the danger is inextricably linked to progress; that it is the price we pay for living in a modern society. What is really meant is that it is the price *someone else* pays.

The poor communities of this nation carry the burden of absorbing the pollution as a result of this complicitous industry-government relationship. There is no evidence of genuine attempts to be fair and equitable in distributing the risks of pollution throughout society. When an industrial plant moves into a community, those who can afford to move out. The only affordable housing remaining is usually in close proximity to the polluting industry and it is the poor who are stranded and forced to remain. It is no coincidence that the polluting industrial plants are in the areas of our cities where people of colour live.

It is no accident that toxic dumps, incinerators and other dangerous facilities are placed in poor, rural areas of my country. A report done by Cerrell and Associates for the State of California provides a blueprint for targeting those communities that have limited power, long lists of problems and economic deprivation. It outlines for industry and government criteria for assessing which communities are least likely to resist the siting of a facility.

Least resistant: small communities, under 25,000 population; rural; employed by facility; sees significant economic benefits; conservative; free market orientation; above middle age; high school or less education; nature exploitive occupations, i.e. farmer, mining; low income. In contrast, those most resistant are: large communities over 250,000; urban; those that live near the facility; don't benefit from facility; professionals; middle or high income; college educated; young and middle age.[9]

Those 'least resistant' have high unemployment and are generally economically deprived and therefore are perceived as being especially vulnerable to the lure of economic development and jobs promised by facility operators and state agencies. Additionally, they are seen as communities with little political clout because they have become disenfranchised from the system.

Studies such as one carried out by the United Church of Christ's Commission for Racial Justice provide evidence that racial and economic factors dictate siting decisions. This showed that 40 per cent of the nation's landfill capacity is concentrated in three communities that have overwhelmingly large minority populations: Emelle, Alabama—78.9 per cent black; Scotlandville, Louisiana—93 per cent black; and Kettleman City, California—78.4 per cent Hispanic. In fact, the size of minority populations living in communities with commercial hazardous waste facilities is five times greater than in those without such facilities because these communities are viewed as easy targets.[10]

The recent obscene attempts to site dumps and incinerators on Native American lands have not been made because our treaties with Native Americans granted them land with special, unique geology that would make the reservations most suitable as dumps. Rather, the reservations are targeted because their populations are viewed as the least able to fight back in our system.

Clearly class, race and ethnicity in a community are driving factors in site selections. Also, in gathering data, the differential impact of pollution on women is never considered. None of the studies that have emerged regarding the inequities of pollution focuses on gender. It seems that just as the feminisation of poverty has been documented, so too should the feminisation of pollution.

The old environmentalism's role

Twenty years ago, George Wiley, an American civil rights leader, told the crowd at Harvard University's Earth Day rally:

I'd like to share with you some concerns that I have about the movement around the environment.... If you are a serious movement, you must be prepared to take on the giant corporations who are the primary polluters and perpetrators of some of the worst conditions that affect the environment of the country and indeed the world ... [but] it has been my experience that most of you aren't going to deal with the problem at the level that it is going to help the welfare recipient, the poor person in the ghettos and the barrios. Most of you are not even going to listen to the voices coming from those communities. You won't ask what they want, and how they want to deal with the problems of their environment, or indeed whether they want to deal with the problems of environment at all—because they feel there are other more pressing priorities in their lives.[11]

The environmental movement in the United States did not heed those words. Instead it excluded from the decision-making process large segments of the population usually those most directly and severely affected. In its isolation it defined the problem, segregated issues, outlined the agenda and identified 'solutions'. That these ignored women, children and the poor should not be surprising.

Mainstream environmental organisations from the Sierra Club to the World Wildlife Fund and Environmental Defense Fund have become part of 'the system' where being 'reasonable' is the driving force, and there is little consideration of the impact on people. These organisations are staffed primarily by scientists, lawyers, economists and political lobbyists. Although many may have an adversarial relationship with agencies such as the EPA, their differences are frequently of degree rather than substance, with an emphasis on tightening or enforcing existing laws rather than developing new approaches. The short-sightedness of these environmental groups, in being concerned with 'controlling' rather than 'preventing' pollution, has encouraged the earth's continued destruction.

These groups have failed also to understand how various issues, such as ozone depletion, acid rain, toxic wastes, and harmful pesticides, are interconnected and are really manifestations of a single, larger issue—the massive production of man-made chemicals by the petrochemical industry. That failure has led to our inability even to begin to address the real problem and to find real solutions. By avoiding identifying the larger issue as the underlying cause of each of the various environmental hazards, we continue to respond in a crisis mentality, bouncing from one trendy issue to the next.

In addition, the United States environmental movement has become an elite group of do-gooders that believes it knows what is best for others: this group of people practises a particularly offensive mode of advocacy that is patronising at best and degrading at worst. The established movement makes decisions and negotiates compromises for others while remaining isolated from the people who actually live where the hazards are greatest.

The mainstream environmental movement has dealt with our communities in much the same way as the United States government has dealt with Third World countries—coming in with a pre-defined agenda, and outlining 'western' solutions, rather than assisting people in fighting their self-determined battles in ways that meet local needs. The communities dealing with the problems caused by toxics have been treated as the 'poster children' to be put on display for white, male-dominated organisations working on single issues.

What makes CCHW different from the old environmental organisations? Maybe because it is rooted in the struggles at the grassroot level where the problems are. Maybe because CCHW continues to be one of the only national environmental organisations led and primarily staffed by women.

And maybe because through all its activities, CCHW stands for the rights of people to have control over their lives, to speak for themselves, and to have a meaningful role in the decisions that affect them.

Los Coyotes—a case study

How does CCHW's approach to building the Movement for Environmental Justice work? How do we help people help themselves? The interaction between Los Coyotes and CCHW was typical of campaigns where CCHW has assisted groups facing a problem.

In April 1990, the Los Coyotes Band of Indians in southern California was contacted by a company called Chambers Development Company wanting to establish a solid waste landfill on their tribal land. Chambers offered to pay the members USD 5,000 per month, for exploratory drilling to be conducted by the company. The drilling would reveal the location of underground water sources, and the Band was promised that if any existing water sources were found too close to the surface, or if there was any danger of contamination, the dump would not be established.

Since that time a lease for a landfill was supposedly signed by the tribal chairman which would waive the Band's sovereign immunity and encumber tribal lands for 25 years. The members of the Los Coyotes Band never saw or approved this lease, nor did they agree to any of its terms. The Bureau of Indian Affairs issued a permit to Chambers to pursue an Environmental Impact Study, which would include conducting tests through dynamite blasting, which was not authorised by the Band.

CCHW received a call from members of the Los Coyotes Band in early 1991, asking for information on Chambers and on solid waste landfills and for any suggestions we might have on how to stop this proposal. They, like most communities, were led to believe that it was too late, that there was nothing they could do to stop the project. We sent information both on the company and on landfills and began to talk them through the issue. We wanted to discover what their concerns were, who was making the decisions, and how other members felt about the proposal. We asked them where they thought they had most influence, in Washington, D.C., with the Bureau of Indian Affairs or on their own land with the Tribal Council? In thinking through the issues and analysing their own strengths, the members saw that they had the most power with their own people, through their own local political process. CCHW simply helped them to recognise their strengths, to develop confidence in their own common sense and abilities, and to think through a strategy.

With that support, members of the Los Coyotes Indian Band organised to form the Coalition for Indian Rights, which has focused on stopping the landfill. To tie them into the network we put them in contact with other groups fighting Chambers or other landfills and with other Native American groups experienced in dealing with these issues. This 'mutual aid' approach, of having experienced people help new people, provides the strength and foundation for the network of activists. It also helps develop leadership as those who have won their battles share their trials and tribulations with others.

On February 10, 1991, the General Council membership of the Los Coyotes Band directed the Tribal Chairman to stop all activities related to the landfill project until members had received a copy of the lease. The Council also ordered that Chambers be prohibited from coming on to the reservation until a decision had been made regarding the landfill. Chambers responded by bringing a private security force on to the reservation to continue their blasting and testing, with written permission from the Bureau of Indian Affairs and in cooperation with the local Sheriff.

This action infuriated the members, who confronted the survey crews and ordered them off the reservation. Members removed the surveyors' stakes and ultimately made Chambers leave. The group then circulated petitions calling for the contract to be voided and for the Band members to rally together and throw Chambers out. By August, 1991, through the efforts of the Coalition, the Tribal General Council members passed a resolution closing the reservation to any landfill development. The Coalition for Indian Rights is now expanding its work to help other Indian tribes keep their lands clean.

The movement for environmental justice

Through this approach, CCHW has helped to create a genuine, new social justice movement—the Movement for Environmental Justice. This movement fights for a clean and healthy place to live and work in. CCHW concentrates on serving the people in our society who are working class and poor; ethnic and racial minorities; in places that other national groups tend to ignore. In ten years CCHW has grown to serve over 7,000 volunteer, grassroots groups and 18,000 individuals, dealing with a variety of waste and toxics issues.

Our approach to change works. In early 1990, a Vice President of Union Carbide was caught circulating an internal memo calling CCHW 'one of the most radical coalitions operating under the environmentalist banner'. This officer urged other Union Carbide executives to take notice because CCHW's 'agenda [would], if accomplished in total, restructure US society into something unrecognisable and probably unworkable. It is a tour de force of public policy issues to be affecting business in year [sic] to come.'[12] What he did not realise was that this 'agenda' that included such revolutionary ideas as: '... no land disposal of materials harmful to life; ... demand prompt and thorough cleanup and compensation for existing toxic messes;

... demand the rights to both jobs and health ...', was the Platform of the Movement for Environmental Justice, developed by over 1,000 people from all walks of life at CCHW's Grassroots Convention in 1989 in Arlington, Virginia. When confronted with the memo the executive apologised, and explained his attempt to smear CCHW: 'It is perhaps an indication of how effective your organisation has become that I felt constrained to use the strongest possible terms.... If we did not believe that at least some of the agenda were achievable, we certainly would not be concerned.'[13]

The corporate response to grassroots efforts

In 1990, CCHW's approach to change and the movement's effectiveness were clearly demonstrated when McDonalds, the worldwide, fast food restaurant corporation, announced it would end its use of styrofoam packaging. It took three years and three months, but the campaign against McDonald's styrofoam packaging that we launched and coordinated in 1987 was successful because it involved people in their own communities. Thousands of groups participated from across the country. CCHW furnished information on the problems with styrofoam, from its ozone-depleting CFC base, to its non-degradation in landfills. We supplied ideas for actions, such as having a group of people go to McDonalds and order their food but demand that those serving them 'hold the toxics' by wrapping it in non-styro packaging; and we connected groups together. We declared certain dates to be 'Days of Action' so groups around the country could do something locally in their own community and know that other communities were also doing something. This gave a national angle to the local campaigns and attracted national press coverage. We were victorious because the McToxics campaign allowed groups to bring the problems of the ozone hole, toxic waste and solid waste, which are all aspects of America's waste crisis, into perspective in their own communities.

The fact that we won may not be as interesting as the approach to the campaign. The McToxics campaign was a successful demonstration of how the movement can have an impact on the 'big picture' without taking people out of their own communities. People in the movement learned that they can have a dramatic effect on public policy without leading a massive march on the McDonalds headquarters (a national event), but rather through a 'nationwide' campaign that focused on the big picture from the perspective of a local community. The McToxics Campaign demonstrated the slogan, 'Think globally—act locally' in its truest sense. The nationwide campaign allowed groups to use the McDonalds case to emphasise their own issue; groups working on a landfill could point to the company's excessive packaging and how it fills existing disposal space and adds to the crisis. Incinerator foes could assert that toxics are released when styrofoam is burned.

Everyone had an angle to emphasise in accordance with the specific concerns of their community.

Nationwide actions also meant that McDonalds could not pinpoint the pressure in the same way as if there had been a demonstration at their headquarters. Their public relations department could not dismiss the action as just a publicity stunt by a small group of wild-eyed, radical environmentalists. The local actions were done by McDonald's own customers—local people who frequent the restaurants. And the pressure was intensified by the managers of the local franchises calling the headquarters wanting to know how to handle the local protests.

In addition the campaign initiated a ripple effect. Children started demanding that their schools stop using styrofoam. Cities passed ordinances against styro-packaging. It was happening locally, in our towns, through our own people, and constantly involving more and more people from all walks of life. It is that local pressure that has changed our lifestyle and made it socially unacceptable to use styrofoam.

The groups we serve win. We document at least 50 tangible victories a month in our journal *Everyone's Backyard*; victories that include not only blocking new unsafe facilities, but also closing old dumps and other pollution sources, testing land, air, water, and health, and receiving new sources of clean, safe water.

Where do we go from here?

Our attempts to force corporations to deal with their waste by 'stopping up the toxic toilet' are working. Because we have made it impossible to find a cheap, easy way to ship wastes 'somewhere else' in the US, we have forced the discussion from *where* toxic wastes should go to *how to reduce toxic wastes*. The next step is to stop the use of toxic substances and our reliance on poisons within our everyday lives. Do corporations have the right to produce whatever they want with whatever poison they choose to create and use? Knowing the burden toxic substances place on our people and our planet, we say no!

In order to push the discussion further, from waste reduction to reducing the use of toxic chemicals, the next loophole must be closed—the exportation of wastes from the industrialised countries to the Third World. As long as corporations have somewhere else to ship toxics the problem will not cease. The communities of the Third World are clearly the next targets for the pollution generated by corporate greed.

We are beginning to see the search for cheap, easy dumping in the Third World. In Papua New Guinea, Global Telesis has attempted to dump toxic wastes. Fifteen thousand tons of toxic industrial incinerator ash from Philadelphia were dumped on the Guinean island of Kassa, killing a large part of the island's vegetation. Haiti received 13,000 tons of toxic incinerator ash also from Philadelphia. Up to 4,000 metric tons of chemical and possibly radioactive waste from Italy were dumped in the port of Koko in Nigeria. New firms have appeared and started to specialise in waste disposal in Third World countries. One such firm run by two men based in New York, the Colbert brothers, stored huge volumes of outdated pesticides, industrial chemicals and solvents in warehouses to be sent to India, South Korea and Nigeria. US agencies such as the Department of Agriculture, the Environmental Protection Agency and many city governments have asked the Colberts to handle their wastes.[14]

Expanding the network internationally

Can the successes we have seen in the Movement for Environmental Justice and CCHW's approach to organising expand to meet this threat? Can we link the organisations throughout the Third World with the US Movement for Environmental Justice in a way that empowers both without overpowering either? We believe it is not only possible and desirable, but an absolute necessity for the survival of us all.

CCHW has certain constraints in our work with others. But those principled constraints are also our strengths. The fact that we will not go where we are not invited limits where we are, but also ensures we will not interfere uninvited, creating more problems for local people. Our approach of helping people help themselves means we will not do things for people that they can do for themselves, but it also helps develop independence and leadership. CCHW will not be an advocate, or speak for others, because we believe people are perfectly capable of speaking for themselves. This builds confidence and skills and allows people to receive the credit they rightly deserve.

With those constraints in mind, we see CCHW's possible role as a conduit for information and support between the people in the US and the Third World. We hope that through linking our networks, exchanging information, and coordinating campaigns, we can be as successful abroad as we have been at home.

Linking our members with groups in the Third World can be accomplished fairly easily. Through contact with our offices, names of groups fighting specific problems and corporations are readily available. We do that now with groups in Europe, Puerto Rico and Mexico. It is simply a matter of establishing a method for communicating the information between the North and South.

Providing background information on corporations and their crimes in the US is also easy. We routinely track corporations throughout industrialised countries, since companies are continually bought and sold between Japan, Germany, France and the United States, making them transnational corporations. Corporate criminals do not recognise national boundaries. Exchanging information on the activities of corporations in both the US and Third World countries will make our data more complete and enable all of us to use their complete records against them.

Another area that CCHW could be of assistance in is an international campaign. As successful as the McToxics Campaign was nationally, a similar international campaign on a selected target could be very powerful. It would require a great deal of communication and coordination, but is clearly possible.

It is clear that a strong social justice movement is alive and well in the United States. As we have seen with the McToxics campaign, the energy spent locally can lead to major changes in public policy and societal norms. This movement is different from many others because it is being directed by the people. We need to fight our battles and expend our energy locally to change the balance of power and to wrest it from the corporate decision-makers. We also need to change the approach of our elected officials in order to give voice to those not usually empowered to speak. At this point, the movement is so vibrant and diverse, that centralising it could destroy it. But expanding it to the people of the Third World can bring new life, energy, and momentum needed for any growing movement. That expansion can give it a power and potential for change rooted in local communities, while shaking the very core of corporate influence.

A revolution is in the making, a restructuring of the seats of power. And at the core are the women of America; the 'hysterical housewives' who wear that title as a badge of their courage. As Cora Tucker, a Black woman in the South says, 'You're exactly right. I am hysterical. When it comes to matters of life and death, especially mine, and my family's, I get hysterical.' The women activists in the Movement for Environmental Justice are proud of the energy and emotions they put forth in these battles. They know it is their passion and strength that enables them to confront the power bases in our country; to stand up in general assembly meetings and demand their right to clean water; to take to the streets and protest against corporate actions that contaminate their families; to find new and creative ways to confront, ridicule, and challenge policies that endanger their children's health and the safety of their communities. We welcome the opportunity to unite our efforts and our network with those of the courageous women throughout the world challenging the powers that be.

The hope for a better future lies with these women ... long live the hysterical housewives of the US and their sisters in the Third World.

Notes

1. Ryan, William, and Schrąder, Richard, *An Ounce of Pollution Prevention: Rating States' Toxics Use Reduction Laws*, National Environmental Law Center, Center for Public Interest Research and Center for Policy Alternatives, January 1991.
2. *The Toxics Release Inventory, A National Perspective*, United States Environmental Protection Agency, (EPA 560/4-89-005), June 1989, p. 1.
3. *Cleaning up: Superfund's Problems Can Be Solved*, US Congress, Office of Technology Assessment, Washington D.C., US Government Printing Office, 1989.
4. *Exporting Banned and Hazardous Pesticides*, Foundation for the Advancement in Science and Education (FASE), Park Mile Plaza, 4801 Wilshire Blvd, Los Angeles, CA 90019, 1991.
5. Stanley, John S., 'Broad Scan Analysis of the FY82 National Human Adipose Tissue Survey Specimens: Volume 1—Executive Summary'. Prepared for the Office of Toxic Substances, US Environmental Protection Agency, Washington D.C. (EPA-560/5-86 035), December 31, 1986.
6. Occidental Petroleum Corporation, Internal Memo, To: D.A. Guthrie, From: J. Wilkenfeld, Subject: Re-entry to DBCP Market, December 11, 1978.
7. Bonn, David, 'Smelter firm put price tag on lead risk', *Spokesman Review,* Spokane, Washington D.C., August 3, 1990, pp. A1 and A6.
8. Nelson, Lin, 'The Place of Women in Polluted Places', in Diamond, Irene (ed), *Reweaving the World: The Emergence of Ecofeminism*, Sierra Club, 1990.
9. 'Political Difficulties Facing Waste-to-Energy Conversion Plant Siting', Cerrell Associates, Inc., 320 North Larchment Blvd, Los Angeles, CA 90004, for California Waste Management Board, 1984.
10. *Toxic Waste and Race in the United States,* The United Church of Christ, 1987, p. 16.
11. Wiley, George, 'Address at Harvard University Earth Day Rally', April 26, 1970.
12. Union Carbide Corporation, 39 Old Ridgebury Road, Danbury, CT 06817-0001, Memo, Public Affairs Group, To: R.M. Berzok, et al, From: C.H. Greenert, Subject: Citizen's Clearinghouse for Hazardous Waste, November 14, 1989.
13. Union Carbide Corporation, Public Affairs Group, letter of apology from Mr C.H. Greenert, Vice President of Public Affairs, 1990.
14. *Toxic Terror: Dumping of Hazardous Wastes in the Third World*, Third World Network, 87, Cantonment Road, 10250 Penang, Malaysia, 1989.

Environmental Degradation and Subversion of Health

Mira Shiva

A series of environmental tragedies over the last decade—Minamata, Chernobyl, Bhopal, the contamination of the Rhine with toxic effluents from Roche, the oil spill in the Gulf, etc.—have focused attention on the increasing 'chemicalisation' of the environment; more or less at the same time, the thalidomide, SMON (subacute myelo-optic neuropathy) and DES (diethyl stilbaestrol) tragedies and, more recently, the increasing incidence of iatrogenic disease and pesticide poisoning have dramatically illustrated the growing 'chemicalisation' of the body. Both developments have forced us to realise that health and environmental issues cannot be dealt with in isolation; not only are they intrinsically linked to each other, but neither can be easily solved by a quick technological fix. For pollution today is not merely chemical, it is also biological, social and psychological. The resulting damage, disability, disease and death are totally unwarranted, usually irreversible and hardly ever compensated; the ultimate tragedy is that they are often compounded by exploitative trade practices and heavily weighted research priorities.

To my mind, the problem may be articulated as one of extreme deprivation on the one hand, and of irrational excess on the other. The deprivation is that of *essentials*, such as food, clean and adequate water, air, health care, and safe living and working conditions. The excess consists of bombarding our beings, our lives, and our environment with hazardous gases, chemicals and biological contamination, i.e., irrational and *inessential* toxification. Important lessons in this area of deprivation and excess can be drawn from the experience of the politics of population policies, which has long divided the South from the North.

History has shown that laws can act as a deterrent whereby social conscience and responsibility take precedence over individual profiteering. But where vested interests have ensured an accumulation of power and money, the silence of the tormented is enforced, and that of law enforcers bought. Legal loopholes are given precedence over morality and ethics, and unjust laws are passed, while attempts to enforce controls are scuttled, whether they relate to the Bhopal gas tragedy, the violation of the Baby Food Code, drug dumping or the indiscriminate use of toxic pesticides. Ecological and health hazards cannot be prevented or dealt with unless a collective consciousness is built up among those who are willing to make sacrifices and to live without destroying and exploiting. It is only when enough people have cared and dared that changes have been enforced.

The impoverishment of the poor is increasing worldwide, even as unprecedented power and means of control are being monopolised by a few, through instruments like GATT, structural adjustment programmes, or through a development model which causes debt and dependency rather than benefiting the poor, as it purports to do. As the disparities and inequities grow, as liberal market forces are let loose, we will see more and more people deprived of essentials, and both people and environment flooded with the irrational and hazardous.

Deprivation of essentials

The deprivation of adequate and appropriate nutrition; of safe and adequate drinking water and pure air; and of basic needs including health care, education, employment, the right to safe working and living conditions and to human dignity, constitute a denial of the essentials of a civilised and just society.

The greatest energy crisis today is that of hunger, suffered by millions of poor across the globe, and especially in countries burdened by the debt crisis and reduced food security as a consequence of structural adjustment programmes, which have severely eroded the survival base of the poor.

Iron deficiency

Nutritional deficiency starts very early in life and is manifested as underweight, stunted height and so on. The most common nutritional deficiency amongst women in India is iron deficiency anaemia; 60–80 per cent of pregnant women suffer from anaemia and 20 per cent of maternal mortality is due to it. They live with chronic fatigue, breathlessness on exertion, headaches, and palpitations, often experience heavy bleeding during childbirth and give birth to low birth-weight babies. Iron deficiency anaemia is not only caused by a lack of iron in food or by menstrual loss, but also by common hookworm infection. This is picked up by walking barefoot on soil contaminated with hookworm, due to inadequate sewage disposal.

The inadequacy of technological fixes is illustrated by the case of the National Anaemia Prophylaxis Programme. An evaluation by the Indian Council for Medical Research of this programme costing several million rupees shows its failure significantly to raise the haemoglobin level in the blood of women administered ferrous sulphate, as part of ante-natal care. The haemoglobin level was 11 gm/litre in 88 per cent of those given iron tablets and the same in 87 per cent of those who were not given the tablets. Frequent pregnancies, childbirth and lactation obviously further deplete the women nutritionally, especially when their nutritional reserves are already low.

Iodine deficiency

In iodine-deficient areas—not merely the Himalayan belt, as recognised earlier, but also large tracts of the Gangetic plain which flood annually—the washing away of iodine from the soil along with many other nutrients leads to iodine-deficiency diseases (IDD). Iodine deficiency in pregnant women can result in miscarriages or the necessity for abortion, stillbirths, the birth of cretinous or hypothyroid babies, deaf-mutes, or babies with psycho-motor retardation. In India alone, 120 million people are exposed to IDD and 60 million actually suffer from it. It is well known that if the total population suffers from goitre then four per cent of the babies born will be cretins or mentally retarded. Iodine deficiency is now being identified in other parts of the country where it was not previously considered endemic. Its appearance can probably be attributed to the increased use of pesticides and fertilisers, and to sewage contamination. All these have goitrogenic properties, while thiocyanates in cabbage, ladies finger, etc., decrease the uptake of iodine.

Vitamin deficiency

Nutritional deficiencies that result from an inadequate intake of vitamins are similarly on the increase for a variety of reasons. The prices of natural sources of vitamins—fresh fruits and vegetables—have increased; as cropping patterns change with the cultivation of cash crops for export, as food prices soar and public distribution systems shrink, the nutritional status of the poor worsens. In the last few decades not only has the consumption of pulses per capita decreased, but land under cultivation with pulses and oil seeds has also been substantially reduced. In addition, budgetary cuts in health and education spending and a trend towards the privatisation of these services will only worsen the health status of the poor majority.

General neglect of women's health

The very high rate of maternal mortality in our parts of the world is indicative of the systematic neglect of women's health, not just at childbirth but for several years before and after. Early marriage, early and repeated pregnancies, and the burden of household responsibilities, all take their toll. The solution to unwanted births lies not in bringing more powerful contraceptive technologies into the market nor in adopting more and more coercive population control methods, but in enabling women to take at least some decisions affecting their own lives. In India, the State of Kerala has shown that women voluntarily choose smaller families; this is clearly due, in some measure, to higher female literacy, awareness of rights and a somewhat improved socio-economic status, but it is also a result of land reforms and the introduction of minimum wages and access to basic health care to ensure the survival of children. Indeed, it is not possible to think realistically about a drastically reduced birth rate without first ensuring food and social security for the poorest among the poor.

Systematic neglect apart, women's health is very adversely affected by a range of social and cultural biases and practices which result in common, avoidable gynaecological disorders, sexually transmitted diseases, AIDS, infertility and a very high incidence of anaemia, urinary tract infections and cervical cancer. Women are also frequently in danger of extreme physical violence.

Without a significant change in their health, and social and economic status, exhorting women to have one or two children only, for the sake of making the population control programmes a success, is meaningless. With increasing poverty such a demand becomes even more untenable, particularly as unjust trade and economic policies will only make matters much worse for women. This has been amply illustrated by analyses of the impact of structural adjustment programmes in Africa and Latin America.

Medical technological fixes cannot compensate for the deprivation caused by deep-seated gender bias, poverty and shockingly inadequate health care, primary education, rural sanitation and drinking water. Each of these has a direct bearing on population control, as we shall see.

Lack of clean drinking water

It did not require the study of social and preventive medicine to demonstrate the great importance of adequate and clean drinking water in ensuring good health, and of the nature of water-borne diseases. Medical books had informed us that 70 per cent of all diseases are water-borne and therefore preventable, and that one-third of all paediatric hospitalisations are due to diarrhoea. The cholera epidemic of 1988 in a resettled slum colony of east Delhi is a perfect example of the interconnectedness of environment and health issues.

Inadequately supplied with water by the municipal corporation, slum-dwellers in the colony resorted to using water from thousands of shallow hand-pumps, only 5–10 feet deep, hurriedly installed prior to the previous elections. During the summer of 1988 over 1,000 overflowing septic tanks remained uncleaned. Each toilet had 108 users. The onset of heavy monsoons spread the faecal sludge all over, contaminating the water in the shallow hand-pumps. Had the people had access to safer drinking water, the tragedy could have been averted or at least minimised; and had the infection cycle been broken by ensuring adequate toilet facilities, and collection and treatment of sewage, the disease would not have spread. The question then arises: was the epidemic caused by the contamination of drinking water or by the non-disposal of overflowing sewage? One thing is clear: the area is six to ten feet below the riverbed, requiring a series of pumps and drains to drain waste and sewage water. Most of these were not functioning at the time. Toilet facilities were grossly inadequate; despite the rapid increase in population as a result of rural migration, there had been no improvement in civic amenities, even basics like sanitation and drainage. Maldevelopment continues to erode the environment base in the periphery as well as in the cities.

Growing emphasis on inessentials provide no solutions

The Delhi epidemic of 1988 was just the tip of the iceberg, and the medical response to it was sadly inappropriate. Over 800,000 people were vaccinated within a week during the peak period, at the expense of oral rehydration therapy and containment with antibiotics, *when it is well known that the cholera vaccine has little or no role to play once the epidemic has set in*. Oral rehydration therapy on the other hand has been hailed as the greatest medical revolution of the century. Its use during the Bangladesh war in 1971 in the refugee camps reduced cholera mortality from 31 per cent to two per cent.

Cholera is a water-borne disease of acute onset in which rapid loss of water and electrolytes through vomiting and passing of watery stools can prove to be fatal unless rapid return of fluids is ensured. This prevents the patient from suffering severe dehydration, after which only an intravenous infusion of glucose saline and an intravenous administration of the deficient electrolytes can save life.

But costly commercial preparations of this kind are liable to backfire: written instructions on how to administer them are in English, a language that most people, especially poor women, cannot read or understand, and many of the packs do not conform to standards set by WHO for the combination of glucose, sodium, potassium and bicarbonate. A few years ago, the head of the paediatrics department at a large hospital in South India noted that a majority of the cases of hypernatremia and convulsions in the paediatric ward were of children with diarrhoea, who were given the commercial oral rehydration solutions in wrong doses. Home-made solutions, taught to the mother and given early enough, are a far safer and more efficient remedy than strawberry-flavoured solutions in 'scientific quality packs', administered unscientifically and too late.

Irrational and hazardous anti-diarrhoeals
It is important to deal with the issue of irrational and hazardous anti-diarrhoeals since they flood the market and figure in the prescriptions of a

majority of medical practitioners. Over-the-counter brands of hydro-xyquinoline (Mexaform and Enterovioform, marketed by Ciba Geigy), have been withdrawn, following consumer pressure. Several brands of gut-paralysers (diphenoxylate hydrochloride) which have a very narrow risk-benefit ratio have been linked to toxicity and death in children. Unfortu-nately, because no warnings are carried in regional languages, such medical remedies for diarrhoea can sometimes prove to be very hazardous. Another common antibiotic combination, which the government's own Drug Con-sultative Committee recommended, in 1980, should be weeded out im-mediately, was the fixed dose combination of chloramphenicol streptomy-cin. This was officially banned through a Gazette Notification on November 3, 1988, but different brands continued to be freely sold, as drug manufac-turers managed to get a stay order against the ban. The adverse effects of commonly used drugs, where the side effects are often more serious or more likely to be fatal than the diseases they are supposed to cure, have been high-lighted by rational drug campaigners. Chloramphenicol, once commonly used to treat typhoid (because of its effectiveness and low cost) can cause se-vere bone marrow depression and a fatal drop in white blood cells. When given to small babies it is known to cause 'grey baby syndrome'. Moreover, its over-use or misuse for trivial problems such as viral diarrhoea (for which, incidentally, antibiotics are an ineffective treatment) results in the emerg-ence of drug resistance.

The irony of it all is that while environmental hazards continue to grow, medical solutions for the commonest and fairly well understood medical problems become more and more warped. Thus instead of early and adequate rehydration for diarrhoea and appropriate use of antimicrobials when needed, irrational and hazardous drugs proliferate. They not only de-tract from the main treatment, but have serious side effects of their own, be-sides being economically wasteful.

New vaccines—new technological fixes
The Vaccine Action Programme (VAP) was initiated in India in 1985 as part of the Reagan-Gandhi Science and Technology Initiative. The 9.6 million dollar Indo-US vaccine project, financed by USAID and US Public Health Service, was concluded, bypassing the high-powered biotechnology scien-tific advisory committee set up by the Government of India. The Union Science Minister was ignorant of the details, as was the Science Advisor to the Defence Minister. The Director-General of the Indian Council of Medi-cal Research said categorically that he would not allow any vaccine to be tried on Indians unless it had been approved for use in the US. The priority areas identified for vaccine trials were cholera, typhoid fever, rotavirus, hepatitis, dysentery, rabies, pertussis, pneumonia and malaria, most of which are either water-borne, air-borne or vector-borne.

There has been an exaggeration of the role of vaccines in disease control and a gross underestimation of the risks and hazards of bio-engineered vaccines. It has been estimated that only 23.5 per cent of the decline in mortality due to infectious diseases can be credited to medical intervention; purification of water, safe disposal of sewage and better food and nutrition have been the most significant reasons for disease control in industrialised countries.

Environmentally hazardous releases of genetically engineered organisms
Micro-organisms have always existed in nature with other forms of life and have evolved with animal and plant species. Genetically engineered organisms are not part of this evolutionary process. The exploitation of recombinant DNA viruses as live vaccines increases the probability of initiating major alterations in the genomes of cells, organisms and species throughout the biosphere. They are potentially volatile agents, which can spread new forms of disease and epidemic even as they are being offered as palliatives for old ones.

The environmental hazards of these technologies are well known to scientists and regulating agencies, for which reason regulatory constraints, public protest and court injunctions against experiments feature domestically in the North. Little wonder then that these experiments are carried out in countries with lax legislation and low public awareness. Bio-engineered anti-rabies vaccine trials were held by Wistar, an American bio-engineering company, in Argentina, in 1986, without the consent of the government or people. As soon as the Argentinian government became aware that they were taking place, the trials were terminated. The Health Ministry stated that farm hands caring for vaccinated cows showed a rise in their antibody titres—they, too, had had the live vaccine passed on to them from the cattle. In India, too, the bovine rabies vaccine field trials constitute a part of the Vaccine Action Programme; all documents, plans, specifications, contracts, schedules and other arrangements, with any modifications therein, must be approved by USAID.

Apart from the question of who determines health priorities and the nature and control of research is the issue of the use of live viruses as vaccines. How will the adverse effects of these live organisms released into the environment be monitored when their full dimensions are not even adequately known? When they present themselves—as they did in the case of thalidomide, DES, the Dalkon shield, SMON and estrogen-progesterone drugs cases—who pays the price in terms of suffering, disability and death? There was a time when it was said that the use of antibiotics in veterinary practice would not affect humans adversely, but very soon sensitisation and the emergence of drug resistance were noticed. When hormones such as oestrogen were used in poultry and animals to make them bigger and to increase profits, the public was told there was no danger—until men consuming poultry that had been hormone-treated developed gynaecomastia, i.e. growth of breasts.

The use of the hormone, pitocin oxytocin, in cattle at the time of delivery was found to have been passed on in their milk, and there have been reports of pregnant women aborting following its intake because oxytocin is known to cause contraction of the uterus. The use of chemicals in animals affects human health as they move down in the food chain. In the US in Maine in 1973, highly toxic polybrominated biphenyl (PBB) was added to cattle-feed instead of magnesium oxide, killing thousands of livestock. By the time the public was alerted the PBB contamination had moved down through the food chain.

Animal feed and Bovine Spongiform Encephalopathy

As the demand for animal feed increased with commercialisation, intensive farming spread to include cattle, pigs, ducks, fish, etc.; 'rendering' plants and 'efficiency' were given priority over microbial safety and nutritional value and by the end of the 1980s the rendering industry was deeply entrenched and considered highly successful in financial terms.

It was in late 1988 that there was a major controversy in the UK over the presence of salmonella in eggs. While attempts were made to convince the public that they could not cause typhoid in humans, the controversy was serious enough to end in the resignation of the Health Minister. It was only due to the salmonella-in-the-egg fiasco that the British public learnt that the reason that salmonellasis had spread so widely in chickens, even infecting the eggs, was because the remains of the food animals were returned to the same species in their feed.

It was in late 1985 that the first cases of Bovine Spongiform Encephalopathy (BSE) occurred, and by 1987, the scale of the epidemic was confirmed. In April 1988, Sir Richard Southwood, Professor of Zoology at Oxford, was asked by the Ministry of Agriculture, Fisheries and Food, to advise them on BSE. His report was published in February 1989 and its key conclusion was that, 'From present evidence it is likely that cattle will prove to be a "dead-end host" for a disease agent and most unlikely that BSE will have any implications for human health. Nevertheless if our assessments of these likelihoods are incorrect, the implications would be extremely serious.'[1]

It is now being found that BSE can successfully be transmitted to mice and pigs and has probably infected cats and zoo animals such as antelopes and their offspring. It is quite clear that cattle are not a 'dead-end host'. It was earlier thought that BSE might be caused by the scrapie agent from sheep, and that due to a low degree of infectivity there was little cause for alarm. But it is now thought that 'BSE resulted from the amplification of this type of agent many thousandfold, so that between one to five per cent of cows and cattle in the UK may be infected'. Southwood's recommendation that

carcasses of all BSE-infected animals be incinerated was never implemented and they were dumped in landfill sites where the infective
agents, being exceptionally resistant to heat, can survive for years.

Lessons from Minamata
The contamination of fish in Peru and the subsequent cholera epidemic
there in 1989, and the mercury poisoning which led to the Minamata tragedy
in Japan, are too well known to bear repeating. In both, facts were suppressed, fears were assuaged by falsification of information, and the toxic
threat problem denied. But some lessons may be drawn from the Minamata
tragedy, at least. First, we really know very little about the chemicals that we
use, produce and discard as untreated waste, believing them to be 'safe'.
There are chemical disease entities which do not exist in medical textbooks,
that are recognised only when tragedies have already occurred. Until the
early 1960s, it was widely assumed that elemental mercury emitted or
dumped into the biosphere was not much of a hazard because it does not
react easily with other substances, is quite stable and is only slightly soluble
in water. Since 1907 when the Chissio plant had been built, routine dumping
of the industrial waste in Minamata Bay had continued. While all the industrial waste dumped into the water was in an elemental inorganic form, it was
the more toxic alkyl form, methyl mercury, that was found in the fish in-
habiting these waters.

By 1972 it had been demonstrated in many parts of the world that relatively
insoluble elemental mercury could be transformed into a highly toxic and
soluble form of methyl mercury by micro-organisms living in the sediments
on the beds of natural waterways. This bio-transformed methyl mercury,
when absorbed by fish tissue and consumed by humans and predators,
settled in kidney, liver and brain tissue. Bacteria isolated from human faeces
can methylate mercuric chloride, suggesting that the synthesis of methyl
mercury compounds from mercury present in food can occur in the human
intestinal tract. Dr Hajime Hosokawa, Chissio's own physician, had begun
animal testing on cats after the 1956 outbreak, feeding them Chissio waste;
on October 7, 1959 he noted that after feeding a cat with cetaldehyde wastes
containing mercury, 'it convulsed, salivated and then suddenly whirled at a
great speed, crashing into laboratory walls'. It was a tragic decision on his
part not to publish the results of his findings until he was on his deathbed in
1979. Irreversible and incalculable human suffering and maiming could
have been avoided, since Chissio continued to maintain that insoluble elemental mercury could not make its way into the food chain. In 1958 when
Chissio quietly moved its effluent discharging outlet from the bay to the
river, people along the river contracted Minamata's disease within months.

In 1959 Chissio installed a cyclator waste water treatment unit with great
fanfare. It was hardly used, because Chissio engineers knew of its ineffec-

tiveness, and mercury-laden waste continued to be dumped into the river. Ten years later mercury poisoning broke out in Migata in Central Japan due to the dumping of toxic substances in the Agano river by the Showa Denko company; the victims sued the company and it was only then that a suit against Chissio was also filed by its victims. They fought for four years, demonstrating, picketing, going on hunger strikes. In 1968 Chissio stopped dumping mercury waste into the Minamata bay, not because of its health hazards or the fear of having to compensate victims, but because the use of mercury catalysts in making aldehyde had been rendered obsolete.

On March 20, 1973, Japanese courts ordered the payment of USD 60,000 to USD 68,000 to each victim of the Minamata disease, depending on the severity of the disability and damage caused. In a second agreement, the victims forced Chissio to bear the living and medical costs of each sufferer, to publicly apologise for negligence, and pay out over USD 200 million in damages. Of 1,401 individuals certified as victims of Minamata disease, 353 had died by 1979.

With more stringent environmental pollution controls in the US and Europe, many polluting industries are moving into the Third World. There is a proliferation of pesticide units in India in Gujarat, Maharashtra and Uttar Pradesh, discharging their effluents into the river Ganges. The Bhopal leak was a disaster not only because it caused the death and disability of thousands, but because it made obvious the fact that neither the government nor the state authorities, nor the scientific and medical professionals had a clue regarding the toxicity of the chemicals being used or produced as intermediates and final products. They were completely ignorant of their hazardous effects and of how to manage poisoning if it occurred, and fairly ineffective in preventing and managing such toxic hazards.[2]

The 1988 H acid (chemical used in making of dyes) poisoning case of Bichri (Udaipur) in drought-prone Rajasthan is another case in point. Five companies making this chemical were discharging their effluents into Udaisagar canal. Sixty wells were polluted, making the water undrinkable for a five kilometre radius and up to a depth of 200 feet, and over 500 acres of land were made uncultivable.

The extensive use of pesticides, many of which are banned in their country of origin, has made cultivation more capital-intensive and also seen the adverse effects of pesticides in the food chain. Pesticide resistance is beginning to appear, failed crops make livelihoods perilous, and the consequent indebtedness has led to some tragic fall-outs. In 1987 over 60 cotton farmers in India's prime cotton-growing district of Prakasam (Andhra Pradesh) committed suicide by consuming pesticides.

The accidental ingestion of pesticide caused the Basti tragedy of 1990 when food distributed in recycled pesticide containers was distributed at a wedding. Two hundred people died as a result. Pesticide poisoning cases have also been reported when highly toxic pesticide pellets have been ground with grain for making flour. Reports of thousands of fish in Kuttanad developing sores on their bodies have been received; similar reports have come in from Malaysia and are related to the presence of industrial chemical effluents in rivers.

Unfortunately, this tendency towards potentially dangerous and irrational excess does not stop with chemical pollutants or fertilisers and pesticides. It pervades the thinking of most planners and policy makers in both the Third World and industrialised countries, and is nowhere more evident than in the prevalent discourse on population control.

The politics of population policies

There is a growing number of people which views population control policies as dangerously close to being racist, sexist and imperialist, as well as anti-poor. These individuals and groups are equally concerned about the health of the nation and the health of its people, and are asking some extremely uncomfortable questions for which there are no easy answers. They want to know why so many corporate giants sit on the Board of the International Planned Parenthood Federation—i.e. representatives of Dupont Chemicals, US Sugar Corporation, General Motors, Chase Manhattan Bank, International Nickel, Marconi, RCA, Xerox and Gulf Oil. They want to know why population policies and research in fertility control are supported by the defence wings of certain countries, and why population is seen as a 'security threat' by them, requiring 'stringent action, bordering on subtle coercion of national governments and through them of their people—which in almost every case happen to be the women'. They say, if stringent population policy was an anti-poverty measure, then those countries in Latin America which have had 80 per cent of their women sterilised should have begun to lead a qualitatively better life, rather than become poorer and more deprived. There should have been fewer poor and fewer street children in Brazil, which brought down its birth rate by 50 per cent within 20 years—something its northern neighbours took several centuries to accomplish.

Hunger, poverty, and national indebtedness have worsened dramatically for most Third World countries. Denied social security, the poor in these countries continue to look to their children to provide labour and social security, especially in agrarian societies. Consequently, they look upon solutions which are 'good for them', coming from outside, with doubt and suspicion. For those involved in health work, population control policies have been a double tragedy, first because they *failed to meet women's contraceptive needs* and second because they *eclipsed other necessary health care work*.

India was the first country in the developing world to formulate its National Population Policy in 1951 with the First Five Year Plan. It was centrally planned, financed and monitored, and implemented at the state and local levels in a typically top-down manner. It did not require the statistical evidence provided by the Planning Commission's mid-term evaluation report to demonstrate that the policy was a failure; recipients of the service had been saying all along that it was not meeting their needs. The predictable bureaucratic response was to change the nomenclature from 'family planning' to 'family welfare' and 'maternal and child health'. But the strategies, attitudes and methodology with regard to family planning, and therefore the treatment of women, remained unchanged. Unfortunately, no one was really listening to the people. After all, the foreign expert's solution is always right, especially when it is handed out together with funds. In their view, women were prone to breeding like rabbits, and therefore their fertility had to be curbed.

How different the scenario would have been had the obvious been recognised at the outset: that female literacy, the guarantee of a minimum wage, and social and political awareness, especially in relation to women's status, have a great deal more to do with opting for a small family norm than do technology-centred, coercive population control programmes. Where the former are not ensured and where women are subordinate in everything, from access to food, education and skill development to freedom in decision making, equal wages and access to productive resources, birth rates are always higher. They are high when the survival of children is not ensured, when there is a repressive compulsion to produce male children, when female children do not count. 'Demographic fundamentalism' is what Ashish Bose calls the craze for male children. When women have no easy access to safe and effective contraception, and absolutely no control over their fertility or sexuality, the freedom not to conceive is not in their hands: they do not have the right to say 'No'. It is ironic and tragic for brain-washed, insensitive or desensitised health workers to mouth slogans and dish out accusations, holding the women 'guilty' of producing too many children, when the women themselves have had little or no say in matters related to conception.

No one cared to listen to what the women had to say—listening with sympathy to their problems and constraints was not part of the population policy. Had those whose hearts bleed for the soaring population of India cared to listen, they would have recognised the need to strengthen the hands of women early enough, educationally, economically, and socially so that they could be helped to make choices about conception and contraception.

The insensitivity and dehumanisation of the programme can be seen in its almost total neglect of all other aspects of women's health problems. The incidence of gynaecological problems—trichomoniasis, moniliasis, acute chronic pelvic inflammatory disease, sexually transmitted diseases, cancer of the cervix and urinary tract infection—is significant. A community-based study by Drs Rani and Abhay Bang carried out in Ghadhcharoli, a tribal district in Maharashtra, found that 92 per cent of women were suffering from gynaecological diseases, 52 per cent with symptoms including pain, discomfort, leucorrhoea, and dyspareunia (pain during sexual intercourse).[3] Other health problems related to child bearing, nutritional deficiencies, communicable diseases, infections, etc., also seemed to merit no concern. Only fertility receives sustained attention.

It is well known that maternal mortality in India is shockingly, embarrasingly high, worse than in many poorer nations. It is also well known that 20 per cent of it is related to iron deficiency anaemia and its complications. Most causes of maternal mortality are preventable; why is it then that women continue to be poorly nourished and to die during childbirth? Is child-birth the cause of death, or is the failure to diagnose, prevent and treat the reasons for maternal mortality (all connected with women's status and their access to food, education and health care) responsible? High maternal mortality is just another symptom of a deep-rooted, widely prevalent and socially accepted gender bias which begins at birth and continues until death. Now, with amniocentesis and pre-natal sex determination, it can be seen even prior to birth. If all the money spent on family planning, where 'target setting' resulted in manipulated 'target meeting' attempts, and where the magic of incentives linked with sterilisation made even conscientious health workers neglect spacing methods and other aspects of health care, had been used more judiciously to meet women's needs, the results would have been more encouraging. The focus on meeting targets led to large-scale corruption; statistics were concocted, family planning camps carried out as many tube ectomies as possible, without after-care or accountability, leaving women with complications and a great deal of dissatisfaction. This in itself turned women against sterilisation, and was far more influential than all the propaganda, including the money incentive.

As a consequence of this misguided policy, not only were women deprived of much-needed health care, they were also denied the knowledge and provision of other non-incentive-related and non-terminal spacing methods that were sorely needed by them and by the nation. It is not surprising that when they began to recognise the lack of genuine concern or interest in solving their health problems, and experienced only aggressive and sometimes subtly coercive manipulation, they became alienated from the health care system. No one really cared about how the family planning programmes were run, how satisfied the recipients were and what problems they faced. In such a situation, the failure to achieve any significant drop in the birth rate was only to be expected.

According to Ashish Bose the major reasons for the failure of the family planning programme have been (i) undesirable foreign orientation; (ii) monopoly on the part of bureaucrats; (iii) monopoly on the part of the central government; (iv) sole concern for quantitative targets and their achievement, irrespective of their impact on birth rate; (v) neglect of women's health. Who should be held responsible for the billions of rupees wasted on this futile exercise, undertaken with the guidance of foreign experts and tied foreign aid? If it were just a question of waste, it might have been explained away; what is regrettable is that a sensitively conceived programme, which could have met the genuine contraceptive needs of many women, was never allowed to take shape. The involvement of people is necessary for the success of any programme like this; if the very people on whom its successful implementation depends have been alienated by target chasers (who should have been health-care providers), the loss has to be calculated in more than just monetary terms. The social costs of this misadventure have been tremendous.

If our health services had addressed themselves to women's health problems and their genuine contraceptive needs, women today would have been the greatest supporters of a humane and sensitively implemented family planning programme. It is the failure of our programmes, policies and of governments to respond to their concerns that has made women refuse to participate in a 40-year old attempt to regulate their fertility.

The myth of choice
In a society where a woman has no choice about when and to whom she should get married, when and how many times she would like to conceive, or even how much she should eat while she is pregnant or lactating, and where she is in no position to avail herself of minimal rest from strenuous work in the terminal stages of her pregnancy, does she really have any choice regarding contraceptive methods? Can she be expected to make an informed decision when she has no access to information, when often the only alternative open to her is sterilisation?

A powerful deterrent to using commonly prescribed, non-terminal methods of contraception has been the serious lack of accessible health care. None of the many thousands of women in whom Dalkon shields had been inserted could seek advice or compensation for serious complications, simply because they had no access to their own medical records. Again, when roughly 50 per cent of our people live below or on the poverty line and are nutritionally deficient and prone to infection, insertion of IUCDs in women with gynaecological infection often causes chronic pelvic inflammatory diseases. These in turn can cause adhesions in the Fallopian tubes, which may result in infertility, ectopic pregnancies and so on. When the number of women involved runs into several millions the potential magnitude of the problem is self-evident.

Although policy advisors, policy makers and health officials responsible for implementation utter the usual reassuring rhetoric on the importance and safety of the various technologies, actual experiences belie their promises. The apparently 'successful' vasectomy camps of Kerala, when repeated in Uttar Pradesh, led to tetanus deaths and had to be abandoned; the laparoscopic method of female sterilisation, considered a 'revolutionary step' in our national family planning programme, led to callous over-use of this technology. Air, pumped through bicycle pumps, was used to inflate the abdomen, rather than carbon dioxide. The question then arises: will the use of newer contraceptive technologies be caring, sensitive and objective or will the same callousness prevail because it is intrinsic in a programme which has failed, from the outset, to consider the social reality of our people and their basic need for treatment with care and dignity?

This leads us to a related question: why is most contraceptive research aimed at women? Why is it that when a recognition of the hazards of hormonal contraceptives have made for lower and lower doses of hormones in contraceptive pills in the North, long-acting injectible contraceptives are considered safe and effective for anaemic, malnourished, infection-ridden, underweight women in the South? If a woman in the North voluntarily chooses such a contraceptive, hers may be considered an informed choice. She is usually in good health and if she happens to develop complications, she has access to follow-up diagnosis and proper treatment. At the best of times, this cannot be assumed for the majority of women in the South. Significant menstrual problems are a recognised side-effect of long-acting hormonal contraceptives; in our context, such blood loss in an already severely anaemic woman can compound the problem considerably.

Similarly, what would the effect of the contraceptive pill be on the foetus if it were given to a pregnant woman? The teratogenic effects of hormones have been recognised, and it is unlikely that they are insignificant in the case of long-acting hormonal contraceptives. Fears have been raised by women's organisations and health and consumer groups about an excessive preoccupation with meeting targets without due warning about side effects.

Objections have been raised to the conducting of trials in violation of the Helsinki Declaration of 1964 guiding physicians in biomedical research involving human subjects, which demands informed consent. Public interest litigation has been filed in the Supreme Court of India by several women's organisations who felt that the bias underlying studies undertaken without full ethical clearance would definitely lead to one-sided results which would then form the basis of family planning policy-making.

If growing population is a major health problem, then the hugeness of the market for new reproductive technologies is staggering. It is little wonder that many pharmaceutical companies have been heavily involved in researching contraceptive technology.

Public memory is short, but we would do well to remember the case of Dr Michael Briggs, consultant to the World Health Organisation, and actively involved in the preparation of a technical report series on female sex hormones. Dr Briggs testified to the safety of hormonal contraceptives, thus obliging the pharmaceutical companies in whose pay he was. Dr Isobel Gal on the other hand, who, in 1967, had showed the link between teratogenesis and hormonal pregnancy tests, and warned about the effect of hormonal preparations in pregnancy on the unborn foetus, had her research work abruptly stopped as it was a threat to vested interests and the rapidly increasing hormonal preparations market. She was hounded, criticised and belittled, her work was discredited, but her long and lonely battle warned others involved with women's issues, consumer rights, health and human rights, of the danger of using hormones in pregnancy.

Thalidomide was supposed to be safe for women and unborn babies, as was diethyl stilbaestrol. No one expected children to be born without arms and legs as a result of the use of the former, daughters to develop adenocarcinoma of the vagina in young adulthood, sons with abnormalities in the testes, or the women themselves to develop breast and cervical cancer years later.

The question is not merely one of side effects; it has to do with denial of information; about who benefits and who loses when decisions are made regarding certain technologies; about who controls them and who is controlled by them; who pays in terms of money and who in terms of health; who carries out and who sponsors the research. If certain technological options are challenged today in terms of their safety and increasing external control it is with good reason. Experience has shown that if provided with unbiased information and safe and effective alternatives, women avoid technologies that are hazardous to their health. It has often been said that potentially hazardous contraceptives are less hazardous than childbirth; such a sentiment can only succeed in perpetuating the failures of yesteryear.

If we are serious about an effective decrease in population growth then the approach to the problem has to be more comprehensive and rational Technological fixes alone will not solve the problem; after all, why have anti-TB drugs not controlled tuberculosis or anti-malarials not eradicated malaria? And why have the great Green Revolution and the presence of food reserves not succeeded in removing malnutrition and hunger?

The population conundrum
If an increasing number of women's and health groups across the world are raising their voices in concern it is because they believe that the prevalent understanding regarding population and conventional strategies to deal with the problem remain basically flawed.

Populist population 'education' succeeds in persuading people that the poor are poor because they multiply like rabbits, and that poor nations are poor, because we have too many people. There is never a mention of over-consumption and waste by the few at the expense of the majority, not just by rich nations but by the rich in poor nations. There is never a mention that the new economic order will further increase disparities and indebtedness-inflation, cutting welfare budgets in health and education, increasing privat-isation of such services, removing food subsidies as country after country is forced into structural adjustment programmes. As poverty increases so does social insecurity; the poor and disadvantaged will tend to look for security in numbers, and national governments will use repressive measures to bring them in line.

That the poor and their children can be held responsible for the nation's pov-erty is one of the greatest economic myths of our times; it shifts the focus away from the real roots of poverty and injustice, while aggressively pushing subtly coercive policies on to Third World countries. Ironically, but not sur-prisingly, it is often the propounders of the most coercive population policies who exhibit the greatest 'concern' for women and their welfare. It is no secret that there is a complicity of interests between medical and phar-maceutical research, transnational funding for such research and interna-tional aid policies. The politics of the pharmaceutical and pesticide indus-tries, however, pales into insignificance when the ramifications of existing population policies are recognised.

Increasing populations are today being blamed for environmental degrada-tion at the same time that forests in Sarawak are being cleared for making disposable chopsticks for Japan; and Indonesian forests, for making toilet paper and face tissues. The indigenous peoples in both are made destitute and homeless in their own land. The inclusion of population policies as an agenda item for the UN Conference on Environment and Development in Brazil, 1992, was cause for concern, because it lent credibility to ridiculous claims, such as the pressure of people and cattle on land being responsible for the size of the hole in the ozone layer. It also allowed those guilty of dumping toxic waste and pumping tons of pollutants into the air and water and soil to arm-twist the poor into silence, for daring to raise their voices in protest. How sensible is it for us to import the diagnosis of what ails us and then import the technological solutions for it, without in any way positively or significantly affecting the birth rate, or adequately meeting the health and contraceptive needs of women?

At a time when social action itself needs to be totally redefined, population is rapidly becoming a human rights issue. It is no longer possible to ensure basic needs at the micro-level when policies at the macro-level are geared to just the opposite. Those concerned with questions of justice and equity, and indeed with issues of development, will have to question the very concep-tual basis of strategies formulated elsewhere.

What has made for indebtedness, what are the loans for, who decides the terms and conditions, who is forced into austerity and who benefits from liberalisation; all these are urgent preoccupations, especially when aid is being yoked to population policy. It is difficult to believe that when our sovereignty is being denied in every other sphere, a heavily foreign-funded present-day population policy will have the interests of the 'poor suffering people of India', especially the women, at heart.

Population policy can no longer be one of curtailing the fertility of ignorant, indisciplined Indians. It has to be seen as a consequence of the failure of other policies—economic, education, health, and so on—at a national level, and of gross economic imbalance induced by the biased and unjust trade policies of the rich North. Coercive family planning measures, with or without incentives, peddled and imposed as a panacea for women's health problems, are no longer acceptable, just as technological fixes for environmental hazards are no longer credible.

Notes

1. Lacey, Richard W., and Dealler, Stephen, F., 'The BSE Time Bomb? The Causes, the Risks and the Solutions to the BSE Epidemic', *The Ecologist*, Vol. 21, No. 3, May–June 1991, pp. 117–122.
2. Skjei, Eric, and Whortan, M. Donald, *Of Mice and Molecules: Technology and Human Survival*, Dial Press, New York, pp. 131–41, 1063.
3. Bang, Abhay and Rani, *The Lancet*, June 14, 1989.

Using Technology, Choosing Sex

The Campaign Against Sex Determination and the Question of Choice

Forum Against Sex Determination and Sex Pre-selection

In a world dominated by the scientific mode, Newtonian models for understanding natural and physical phenomena have displaced earlier worldviews, in which religion and the supernatural figured to a greater or lesser extent. Instead of placating such forces, we now endeavour to control them; scientific 'knowledge' is being used to determine and achieve the desired ends.

One dramatic illustration of this is the use of a highly developed technology, amniocentesis, for detecting genetic abnormalities in foetuses and also as a means to determine their sex. Society has hitherto looked to gods and supernatural powers to realise its desire for male progeny; it has now turned to the practitioners of modern medicine.

This is not to say that the shift has been sudden. Traditional systems of medicine and healing have also contributed their share: Ayurveda lists a number of practices for determining the sex of the foetus after conception, and for selection at or after conception. Ayurvedic texts state that the sex of the foetus is determined only six weeks after conception, and therefore may be 'manipulated' prior to this. Pre-selection exists in prescribed copulation postures, times and days; in diet, eating and consumption habits, especially after conception; certain rituals to be performed before and after conception, and so on.

What then do we find so different or shocking about modern allopathic medicine providing fail-safe techniques for sex determination and pre-selection? For one, the fact that they are precisely that: accurate and irreversible. Then, in the security of its modernism and 'neutrality' science reinforces or legitimises conservative, orthodox prejudices. Again, its philosophy has become the dominant mode of thinking in society today, and the belief is that it invests men with more or less full control over lives and bodies. For all these reasons we feel that its 'achievements' need to be examined more closely.

Over the last ten years, efforts have been made to campaign against the practice of sex determination and sex pre-selection. In the following pages, we as members of the Forum Against Sex Determination and Sex Pre-selection (FASDSP) present our perception of this campaign in which we have been active participants as a group for the last seven years. We offer a detailed account of our efforts, a critique of our actions and strategies, an appraisal of our understanding and a formulation of the issues as they emerged in the course of the campaign.

Obviously, our journey has not been altogether smooth. We have consciously and unconsciously shifted lanes according to our understanding or as demanded by the prevailing situation. We wish to share our progress in order to help arrive at an understanding of the commonalities as well as the specificities of all the issues in which we are involved in one way or another.

Our journey begins in 1982

The Government of India brought about a partial ban on sex determination tests in 1976. This followed a protest launched by women's groups against survey results which indicated that an overwhelming majority of couples (90 per cent), who had volunteered for clinical trials at the All India Institute of Medical Sciences in Delhi, were desirous of aborting female foetuses once their sex was known. When the Government banned the tests in public hospitals, the issue was forgotten.

The existence of private clinics offering this test remained more or less unknown, until some national dailies published news and advertisements about a particular clinic in Chandigarh, in 1982. Immediately women's groups from Bombay, Delhi and other places issued a statement against the test. People's science and health groups such as the Lok Vidnyan Sangathana and the Medico Friends Circle, as well as research organisations such as the Centre for Women's Development Studies, Research Unit on Women's Studies, SNDT, Bombay, and the Voluntary Health Association of India joined in the protest, questioning the role of scientists and doctors who helped to propagate the tests.

During this period the emphasis of the campaign was mainly on writing articles in the media, and creating a pressure group by highlighting the issue. The focus of concern was the dangerous effects that these techniques could have, either of permanent damage to the foetus or injury to the woman's uterus. Further, the efficiency of the test was also questioned; indeed, the very information regarding the availability of such testing in private clinics came as a result of a newspaper report of a 'wrong' detection in one, Dr Bhandari's clinic in Amritsar, where a 'male' foetus had been aborted. But when it started to look as if improving the test would eliminate all the problems associated with it, the campaign petered out.

The 'Forum' is formed

In November 1985, a group of activists from women's groups and people's science groups in Bombay agreed on the need for more consistent action in banning the sex determination tests, seeing the extent to which they had spread. After a series of discussions, we came together as a joint action group, the Forum Against Sex Determination and Sex Pre-selection. Keeping in mind that one of the primary weaknesses of the earlier attempts at building up coordinated action was lack of a broader perspective, it was decided that the campaign must consider the issue at multiple levels. The question of sex determination and pre-selection was then primarily seen as: (i) an integral part of women's oppression and discrimination; (ii) a misuse of science and technology against people in general and women in particular; (iii) a human rights issue. Due to the multi-dimensional character of the issue, activists from various social action, people's science, health, human rights and legal action groups, as well as concerned individuals joined in the campaign, along with women's groups.

To handle the technical aspect of the issue, a two-pronged approach was used. All of us, including those with an aversion to science, medicine or any kind of 'technical' stuff, went through the process of understanding the basic techniques. The focus of the campaign, however, was not on their 'goodness' or 'badness', but on the issue of discrimination between boys and girls in all sections of society. Linked to this was an attempt to show that sex determination was yet another form of violence against women, part of the chain made up of female infanticide, wife-burning, *sati**, etc. The threat to the survival of women was itself evident from their declining sex ratio: from 972 females per 1,000 males in 1901, to 929 females per 1,000 males in 1991, a rather shocking statistic.

After long discussions and an initial workshop to equip ourselves with the technicalities (medical, social and legal) of the matter, we set out. An immediate regulation of pre-natal diagnostic techniques was sought, for which, naturally, we had to turn to the legal and state machinery. Simultaneously, we wanted to conduct the campaign so that public pressure could be mounted, and our basic message *Ladki na ladke se kum* (A girl is no less than a boy) could reach the people.

The first problem with regard to framing any regulation was of proving that an abortion was consequent upon a sex determination test; next, one would need to modify the Medical Termination of Pregnancy Act. Not wanting to curtail women's right to abort, we did not pursue this idea for long. The alternative was a new law—the first law of its kind, regulating diagnostic techniques. We had decided not to ask for a total ban because we did feel that the detection of genetic abnormalities was essential in situations like ours, where mothers have to pay such a heavy price for bringing up children with birth defects. But strategically, too, we felt that a demand for a total ban might be squashed altogether.

We formulated the Act as we would have liked it to be and tried to push the

---

* The ritual immolation of a widow on her husband's funeral pyre.

idea through with the state bureaucracy. A sympathetic health secretary and a few contacts in the Legislative Assembly helped the process. Signatures were collected from all over the country and from 'eminent' persons from all walks of life. Lobbying was done with members of the Assembly and others who mattered. Articles were written in the media and events held to highlight the issue, mainly for press coverage, at crucial junctures in this legal campaign. We managed to be represented in the expert committee to formulate such a law. We also had a pilot study done in Bombay on the prevalence of sex determination tests, which revealed the following:

About 84 per cent of the gynaecologists interviewed for the study were performing amniocentesis for sex determination; on an average they together performed 270 amniocenteses per month.

Some doctors had been doing such tests for 10–12 years, but the majority (over 85 per cent) had been doing so only for the past five. About 74 per cent of the doctors said that over half the women who came for the tests were middle class, and more than 85 per cent of the doctors said that they had tested no lower class women, although the areas selected for the study had a substantial lower class representation.

A majority of the women already had two or three daughters, while the percentage of those seeking a sex determination test after the birth of four or more daughters was relatively low. Significantly enough, about 24 per cent of the doctors said that in 20 per cent of the cases, women had only one daughter when they came in for the sex determination test, and 29 per cent of the doctors said that up to 10 per cent of the women already had one or more sons. A majority of the doctors thought the sex determination tests were a humane service for women who did not want any more daughters, and some even felt that they could be an important family planning device for our country.

Lobbying to get the Act passed remained our primary objective at this stage. It helped give us a direction; it helped to raise the issue on various platforms, and it focused attention on the point that we were trying to make.

In June, 1988, the Act came into being in the State of Maharashtra. Although it demonstrated the state's response to the campaign, the Act itself has certain provisions which are clearly counter-productive.

(1) *Punishment for the woman*: According to the Act, a woman undergoing a sex determination test is presumed to be innocent, but is still fined Rs 50; if proved otherwise, she is subjected to imprisonment for three months and/ or a fine of Rs 1,000.

In practice, a woman under severe pressure from her in-laws will tend to internalise blame and accept the punishment, thus making for further victimisation. Meanwhile, the husband or parents-in-law are not held liable. An exceptional woman, who musters up courage to lodge a complaint under this Act, would not dare to do so if she were afraid of being punished by it.

(2) *Granting licences to private labs/clinics/centres*: In Maharashtra, as anywhere else, the granting of licences to private institutions would only le-

gitimise unethical practice carried out by them earlier. Government institutions all over India have been following the ban on the misuse of amniocentesis for the past several years, but not one case of violation of this ban has come to light so far. In Maharashtra, a reputed geneticist was found to be performing this test illegally after the ban and although the news was flashed in leading city newspapers, the government chose to ignore it. As far as the genetic testing for foetal abnormalities is concerned, looking at the number of people who have availed themselves of the facility in Maharashtra, we feel that the infrastructure and expertise available in government hospitals and those attached to medical colleges is sufficient to cater to their needs.

(3) *Prohibiting access to the judiciary*: According to section 21(1) of the Maharashtra Act, no person other than the authorities laid down by the Act can seek the help of the judiciary against any alleged violation of it. The person has to give notice of not less than 60 days to the State Appropriate Authority or State Vigilance Committee in the prescribed format, which is not given in the rules governing the Act. If the committee itself is not formed in time, this clause delays all probability of any action.

(4) *Non-answerability of government machinery*: The various bodies appointed under this Act are not accountable to the public. No punishment is given out to them for failing in their duty; this leaves people with no recourse in the face of repeated negligence on the part of the state.

Despite all its loopholes, however, the Act served to bring the issue into the limelight and it also gave us legal sanction to confront sex determination clinics. We were aware even then that it would not stop clinics from offering the 'facility' altogether; what we hoped for was some restraint because of the illegality that was attached to it.

We were also aware that even a nominal implementation of the Act could take place only if people did not want to avail themselves of these facilities. In the initial stages of the campaign itself, however, we came to the painful realisation that the vast majority of people was not likely to spontaneously support the campaign. We tried our own very general ways of reaching out, of establishing connections between different issues and of emphasising the slogan that we had evolved specifically for the campaign: *Lladki na ladke se kum*. Films were made, songs written, meetings held at various places, and with all kinds of people. Skits were enacted with children, and positive action taken by holding parent-daughter marches and children's day programmes.

Along with this, in April–May 1988, eight organisations jointly organised a fortnight-long programme *Nari jeevan sangharsh yatra* (A quest to liberate women's lives). The focus of the programme was on all the issues related to women's survival. An exhibition, accompanied by a booklet, was set up, linking the issues of female foeticide and infanticide, wife-murder, rape, *sati*. Programmes comprising of videofilms, slide-shows, poster exhibitions, plays, skits, debates, etc., were organised at twelve different places in the city of Bombay.

After June 1988

Up until then, we had been so preoccupied with getting the law passed that we had little time to pause. Not that there were no doubts; having worked on other legal campaigns, we were quite aware of the limitations therein. However, the momentum set by the state administration and the prospect of an Act soon kept us going, forced us into taking some kind of action. The unanimous passing of the Act by the state government made for a sudden slowing down in pace. Central legislation was nowhere in sight and the state bureaucracy was taking its own time to constitute committees, register private genetic clinics and laboratories and so on. We paused too.

We realised that there had been a growing restlessness within all of us about doing the kind of work required for getting legislation passed. That apart, we were most uncomfortable about really not being aware of what people in general felt about such legislation. Coupled with this was the fact that we were asking for more state control over women's lives. On the one hand, we have always been wary of state control, and on the other, the thrust of our campaign had been just this. In fact, in a society where the bias in favour of a male child is so predominant, our unyielding stand against sex determination certainly did not reflect majority opinion. So we had the unpleasant option of going against what the majority of people seems to believe in, and collaborating with the state which, most of the time, is anti-people.

In this situation, where we were forced to work with the state, we had tried to ensure some system of checks and balances. Access to information was one of these. The Act had provided for the mandatory publishing of periodic reports giving details of the number of tests carried out in registered centres, indications that required such tests, and their diagnoses. We tried to pursue this by demanding full access to all documents for members of the vigilance committees and the public. We also tried to get voluntary organisations represented on the former.

The experience of the State of Maharashtra, however, demonstrated the limitations of these suggestions in the face of an unwilling state machinery. No reports have been published to date. Committees took a long time to be formed and voluntary organisations were inadequately represented on them. Almost all the non-government appointees, including representatives from voluntary organisations working with women, are medical professionals. How and in whose favour these committees would work is anybody's guess.

In June 1989, local level committees were formed for all districts except

Bombay, and in June 1992, registrations were given to 24 labs and clinics all over the state, 17 of them in Bombay! No case has been registered under the law so far, and the test is still available in Bombay.

In a sense, state legislation was effective only in marginally reducing the number of clinics and increasing the charges for the tests. In another sense, however, since the Maharashtra Act was passed, interest in the issue has been aroused in the entire country, something that had not happened earlier. Today, joint action forums have been formed in Bangalore, Delhi and several cities of Gujarat. Concerned groups in Chandigarh, Calcutta and Pune are also actively campaigning for an all-India ban on sex determination tests. As a result, three other state governments—Goa, Gujarat and Orissa—announced their intention to introduce similar legislation.

Having waited for a long time the Central Government has also finally introduced a bill in this regard. It has the same major loopholes as the Maharashtra Act, but this time, public opinion has been sought on the bill. A Joint Parliamentary Committee was constituted which has held discussions and dialogues with organisations and people active in the campaign in various cities.

Based on our experiences with the Maharashtra Act, there have been some changes in our stand. We feel today that only those who actually provide the facility should be penalised. We are therefore against any punishment being given to persons seeking the test, whether it is the woman herself or the family who might have persuaded her. In our opinion, the law is meant to regulate the *tests* and to prevent their misuse; thus only doctors or providers of the technique are responsible for their violation. Moreover, the burden of changing the social evil of discrimination against daughters is not the law's alone.

The Central Bill does not envisage any role for voluntary organisations in the vigilance committees; based on our experiences we feel that representation through voluntary organisations is not sufficient—*it is essential that the general public have direct access to information and judicial action.*

The proposed central legislation is in a sense an achievement of the nationwide campaign. The way in which this 'achievement' has been credited to us, and the whole question of democratic principles and values, troubles us. In a way we see a parallel in our use of the law and in the establishment's promotion of technological solutions. Society tries to find solutions to social problems in technological innovations: are we, too, seeking such solutions through the agency of the law? Whenever we ask for reforms in existing laws or the formulation of new ones, are we expecting the government to be on the side of women?

This is the dilemma which confronts all women's groups. Whether it is the Dowry Prohibition Act or Section 498 A of the Indian Penal Code, or the Family Courts Act or the present Act under discussion we do believe that we really cannot rely on these alone or on government to get justice for women. But through the process of campaigning for them, through the protest and pressure generated, more and more women are exposed to diverse views, and a social atmosphere is created which can strengthen women in their struggle. Various groups can forge links and strengthen the movement by reaching out to more women and mobilising public awareness.

At the same time we feel that the demand for, and enactment of, such legislation is one way of making a statement opposing discrimination against women in society. It is necessary that the government be forced to take note of such practices in society, and register the fact that society, represented in parliament, takes serious objection to their continuance. It is also necessary to strip the garb of respectability from such brutal practices through their legitimation by modern medical technology. By making them illegal the tacit, social sanction that they enjoy can be removed.

Our other dilemmas are related to much wider issues. In the campaign we had taken the stand that these pre-natal diagnostic tests needed to be regulated, that they be allowed for the detection of genetic abnormalities, taking into account women's burden as the principal child rearers in our society. Although we have some questions on this point, we still feel, that until society takes collective responsibility for child care we would have to abide by our present stand.

The wider problem of acceptance of new technologies

While campaigning against sex determination and trying to think of how to launch a campaign against sex pre-selection, we were faced with a totally new dimension of the technologies themselves. A series of issues, such as in vitro fertilisation (IVF), gamete intra-fallopian tube (GIFT), and the whole domain of genetic engineering needed discussion. Not all of them could be explained away only as discrimination against women or the misuse of science and technology. We needed to undertake a critique of modern science and technology as well as society's views on all forms of reproduction.

At the conference of the Feminist International Network of Resistance to Reproductive and Genetic Engineering (FINRRAGE) in March 1989 in Bangladesh, the debates left us baffled and bewildered at times. Intervention in nature's biological processes began as early as agriculture. How does one distinguish that intervention from the one made by genetic engineering? Artificial insemination (AI), IVF, hybridisation and so on are techniques that have long been used in farming and cattle breeding. Why is it that we begin to question and protest only when such engineering is proposed for human beings? Is our view genuinely holistic or are we still being propelled by an androcentric urge, the loss of this earth and its environment which is crucial for 'us' human beings?

What does one mean by 'eastern' and 'western' science in today's context? While evolving or trying to evolve a new philosophy of science, how does one accept and understand the knowledge acquired so far? How does one work towards a non-reductionist methodology of science? We surely do not believe in saying a categorical 'No' to technology. Is there a qualitative between difference the various technologies? If so, how does one identify it and, if not, how does one evolve the criteria by which a distinction can be made to help us determine those that are desirable and appropriate and those which are not.

The list of questions is unending and answers are not simple. We also know that they need much more collective thinking. What we fear, however, is that these and similar debates are getting further and further away from the people who are directly affected when technological innovations backfire—witness the gas leak at Bhopal, the control over women's reproduction whether in treating fertility or infertility, and so on. We realise that those of us who have access to information and can afford the luxury of theorising have the responsibility to make this a broad-based debate, to initiate and maintain communication to bridge the chasm. As of now our efforts are far from sufficient.

Finally, there is the question of translating these debates into action. The campaign against sex determination and sex pre-selection is one limited example of these efforts. There are many more scattered all over the country—that question development, that force one to rethink modern science and technology, that identify whose interests are taken care of by what. In all of these a common feature has been that while, in the long term, the effects of environmental disasters are for 'life on earth' itself, in the short term they appear to be a clash of interest between two sections of people.

On the Narmada dam issue, for example, the apparent gain of water for irrigation and power generated, especially for the state of Gujarat, seems to be posited against the loss of people's homes, communities and life-styles. Cost-benefit figures differ because people's notions of costs and benefits differ. But due to the presence of a large number of people who are immediately affected, will suffer loss and do not benefit in any way from a project like the Narmada dam, there exists a broad people's base to the struggle against it.

The case of reproductive technologies, however, is slightly different. Here, typically, women are often compelled into accepting a harmful, dehumanising technology in a no-choice situation, where it seems to offer a viable solution, at least to their immediate problems. To a woman who is not allowed to use contraception and who is unwilling to shoulder the burden of repeated pregnancies, deliveries, miscarriages and abortions, an invisible injection/implant can be a solution; to a woman who has been branded barren, IVF can be a solution; to a woman whose only recognition is as a producer of sons, sex determination and sex pre-selection become solutions. All of these are important also because they give the illusion of bringing about a change in one's situation.

At the Forum Against Sex Determination and Sex Pre-selection, while continuing with our single issue campaign, we are broadening out to include specific action against other reproductive technology. In a sense, this is an attempt to evolve other methods of campaigning which may be more effective than the one chosen earlier. Today, we are at the stage when we are aware of the achievements and limitations of the earlier part of our campaign, yet unsure of where to turn next. What keeps us going is the commitment to persevere and move on, and to do so individually and collectively.

Legal Rights ... and Wrongs: Internationalising Bhopal

Indira Jaising and C. Sathyamala

The Bhopal disaster

The disastrous event on the night of December 2, 1984, in Bhopal, in which more than 40 tons of a deadly mixture of toxic gases from the Union Carbide factory escaped into the atmosphere, has been misleadingly termed an accident. In fact, the disaster which killed thousands and injured several million permanently, could almost have been predicted. In the late 1960s, a decision was taken at the Union Carbide Corporation (UCC) headquarters in the US to set up a factory for the manufacture of pesticides in a populous section of the city of Bhopal, capital of the state of Madhya Pradesh in India. The nature of the product, the process of manufacturing, the secrecy surrounding all procedures, the double standards in safety maintained by the transnational company, the measures taken by the management to cut costs, the run-down condition of the plant, all added up to create the right mix for a massive environmental disaster.

That it was just waiting to happen had been noted by a Bhopal-based journalist, Raj Kumar Keswani, three years before December 1984. In a series of articles printed in *Saptahik Report* (The Weekly Report), a local Hindi newspaper, he wrote, 'Save! Please Save the City', 'Bhopal on the Mouth of a Volcano', and 'If you don't understand you will be wiped out'. (September/October, 1982.) Again in June 1984, barely five months before the disaster, he underlined his warning in an article published in a Hindi daily, *Jansatta*. Today, the corpses of the dead and the suffering of millions stand in mute testimony to the prophetic nature of his warning, which was based on a study of the total absence of safety mechanisms in the manufacture of a deadly chemical.

The Bhopal disaster had the potential for changing the face of the entire chemical industry and for challenging the need for technologies that can cause grave and irreversible damage to the environment and to people. That it has not, only demonstrates the utter contempt industry has for life in its all-consuming pursuit of profit. An analysis of the response to the disaster will help to unravel the nexus between a transnational corporation and a national government and its agencies in their combined effort to suppress and underplay the magnitude and consequences of the event. It is almost as if they have succeeded in erasing the event from human memory and public consciousness.

The failure of transnational corporations

The catastrophe demanded from the Union Carbide Corporation, the organisation responsible for the accident, a response that was humane and in keeping with the image that industry wishes to project, that of a concerned partner. The immediate task was to provide medical relief to the thousands of exposed victims who flooded the hospitals in Bhopal. As people were brought in, the management of the factory maintained that the gas was non-poisonous, that it was 'just like tear gas' and that its effect on the eyes could be relieved by washing with water. Medical experts flown in by Union Carbide assured the Bhopal victims that recovery was almost certain and that there would be no long-term effects from the exposure.

Further, the Union Carbide Corporation refused to reveal the composition of the gases in the gas cloud, the toxicological information on these gases, the nature of injuries that could be caused by exposure and the antidote or specific treatment which needed to be prescribed. Even Dr Bipin Awasi, Medical Director and Toxicologist at the UCC plant in the US, retracted his earlier statement about the possibility of cyanide poisoning. It was only when it became clear that UCC was not going to respond positively that a litigation strategy began to be worked out.

The failure of legal mechanisms

The first legal response came from American lawyers who flew down to Bhopal and obtained thumb impressions from the victims, authorising the lawyers to file suits on the victims' behalf in the US. Some of these attempts were so crude that there were reports of authorisations being available at a price. Based on these authorisations, suits were filed in different states in the US, and all were subsequently transferred to the Southern District of New York to be judged by Judge Keenan. It was at this point that the Indian government woke up to the situation and attempted to formulate a legal strategy. Its response was to enact a law which gave the government the sole authority to litigate on behalf of the victims. Armed with this new Act, the Bhopal Gas Leak Disaster (Processing of Claims) Act, 1985, the Indian government filed a suit in the Southern District of New York, to be heard along with all the others. Even while these suits were pending, negotiations had begun on settling the dispute, well before anyone had had an opportunity to estimate the nature and extent of injury, the number of dead and injured and the long-term consequences of the disaster. The American lawyers proposed a settlement of 350 million US dollars; although there was no rational basis for this amount, Judge Keenan was invited to accept it as fair. Reports say the Union of India (UOI) refused to accept the settlement not because it was opposed to it in principle, but because it was dissatisfied with the amount. It is not clear why it opposed it, nor is there any record of whether it had proposed an alternative figure for consideration.

In the absence of consent to the settlement on the part of the Union of India, Judge Keenan had to proceed with the hearings. At this stage, UCC made an application to the court that the suits be dismissed on grounds of forum and convenience. Simply stated, what was being argued by UCC was that the US was an inconvenient forum in which to decide the suit, the inference being that it should be tried in India since all the evidence and witnesses were located there. The hidden agenda was, quite clearly, UCC's wish to avoid paying the levels of compensation ordinarily awarded by US courts in tort litigation; secure in their assumption that life in India was cheap they were confident that an Indian court would make much lower awards. Judge Keenan accepted the arguments of UCC and transferred the case to India on condition that UCC submit to the jurisdiction of the Indian courts, which they willingly did. His decision reflects the political reluctance of the American legal system to deliver justice to people of Third World countries who have been the victims of American transnational corporations. It seems clear that neither the voluntary groups in India, who strongly favoured conducting the litigation in the US, nor the UOI had anticipated this decision. As a result, both were caught off-guard, fumbling to formulate a strategy for pursuing the litigation in India.

By this time the American lawyers had already lost interest in the case, and the pitch was therefore clear for the Indian government to become the sole representative of the victims within the authority of law. Strangely enough, none of the groups of victims that had been formed by then realised the enormous implications of surrendering vital decision-making powers to the UOI, which now assumed the role of *parens patriæ* vis-à-vis the victims. No attempt was made to challenge the exclusivity of the government's right to represent the victims; they now lost round two of the legal battle, this time to the Union of India.

One solitary petition was filed in the Supreme Court in early 1986 by Rakesh Shroti, an advocate, a resident of Bhopal and a victim of the tragedy, who challenged the validity of the Act, claiming the right to be represented by lawyers of his own choice and stating his apprehension that conceding exclusive powers to the government would mean giving them the right to settle or negotiate the claims with UCC, without the knowledge of the victims.

Meanwhile, the suit was being litigated in the district court of Bhopal, with UCC doing everything in its power to delay the proceedings. At this point, one of the victims' organisations, Zahreeli Gas Khand Sangharsh Morcha (Forum Against Toxic Gas Poisoning) made an application for interim relief to be provided to the victims; it was supported by the UOI but vehemently opposed by UCC. However, even this application did not contain any details of a realistic estimate of the number of people injured and the nature and extent of their injuries.

The failure of the medical system

The logical consequence of the legal appropriation of the disaster was its medical appropriation as well. Government research units such as the Indian Council of Medical Research (ICMR), the Defence Research Development Establishment, the Industrial Toxicology Research Centre and others were given an exclusive right to conduct epidemiological surveys and toxicological research and to suggest possible lines of treatment. They failed to associate voluntary organisations or any victim groups with this effort. As a result, the medical aspect of the disaster was gradually, almost deliberately, shrouded in secrecy. All information was made confidential under the Official Secrets Act. Because of the monopoly on medical information, it was virtually impossible to keep vested interests in check, and the consequences of this appropriation were a minimising of the nature and extent of injury and a failure to come up with the required line of treatment for the victims. The ICMR took almost three months to suggest that a course of sodium thiosulphate injections (NATS) be given to the victims. NATS is a specific antidote in cyanide poisoining and had been suggested by Dr Bipin Awasi, the Medical Director of UCC in the period immediately following the disaster. It was opposed by UCC and a section of the medical community in Bhopal which maintained that the effects of the gas were felt only in the eyes and lungs and that NATS would provide no symptomatic relief. Although this debate was posed as a medical controversy, a conflict between two contradictory medical opinions, it was in fact political. While it is true that the ICMR failed to provide further proof of the efficacy of NATS, the debate had more to do with demarcating the extent of injury. Accepting NATS as a treatment would have meant acknowledging that the toxic gases had indeed crossed the lung-blood barrier to cause systemic damage. The controversy ultimately led to the withholding of NATS from the victims, and now it is too late to determine whether it would have provided any relief to them had they received it in the early exposure period.

The State: protector of victims versus mediator of foreign investment

The appropriation of medical information meant that the medical consideration was subordinated to the political one. There was a clear conflict of interest between the demands for justice for the victims, and the need of the Indian government for foreign capital. A proper epidemiological study which could have been the turning point in establishing the nature and extent of injury was not undertaken and, until today, no proper scientific survey of the entire exposed population exists. The confusion about treatment was never resolved. The teratogenic, carcinogenic and mutagenic potential of the gases was denied without adequate proof. Thus even at the point when the Indian government filed its suit for three billion dollars in the US, no valid survey of the gas victims was available. So the government gave arbitrary figures for the number of those injured, and these ultimately became the basis for the interim order passed by the Bhopal district court for Rs 350 crores (approximately USD 115 million) to be paid by UCC; the High Court later reduced this to Rs 250 crores (approximately USD 85 million). It was this interim order that UCC challenged in the Supreme Court of India, exposing their strategy of delaying monetary relief with the sole purpose of arm-twisting the victims into an unfair settlement.

For five years no monetary relief from any source was made over to the victims. Then, on February 14, 1989, they were told that a settlement had been reached: the Union of India and Union Carbide had agreed on a figure of USD 470 million in settlement of all claims past, present and future, and to quash all criminal charges against UCC. This settlement created national and international outrage at the blatancy of its disregard for the injury caused to the victims, and at the Indian government's sell-out to a transnational corporation.

The Supreme Court of India gave its endorsement without even adjudicating on the validity of the Bhopal Act under which the government had arrived at a settlement. Realising this blunder, in March 1989 it decided to hear the petition challenging the Bhopal Act, while the settlement itself was held in abeyance. Union Carbide, aware that there was a strong national sentiment against the settlement, quickly transferred the USD 470 million to India so as to present the court with a *fait accompli*. In the meantime, review petitions were filed by organisations such as the Bhopal Gas Peedith Mahila Udyog Sanghathan (The Association of Women Victims of Bhopal) and several others, challenging the settlement. Even at this stage, UCC's strategy was to sidestep the issue, but it was ultimately directed by the court to continue to submit to the jurisdiction of Indian courts until the validity of the Act and the settlement were decided.

Ultimately, in December 1989, the court delivered its judgment by upholding the Act and the power of the government to settle the dispute, but made a very important contribution to the cause of the victims by stating that they had a right to be heard before any settlement could be arrived at, and acknowledging the fact that they had not yet been heard. It also said that the UOI was obliged to pay interim relief to the victims since they had assumed the responsibility of litigation on their behalf.

It was while the interim relief petitions were being heard that the victims were confronted by the gross under-estimation of the nature and extent of injury and the number of those injured, as assessed by the Madhya Pradesh government.

Conflicting assessments of injury

In January 1987, two years after the disaster, the Madhya Pradesh government, in order to provide medical documentary evidence for all the claimants in the case against the UCC, initiated the process of assessing personal injuries for approximately 600,000 persons who had filed compensation claims. Two years later, in 1989, after the process of medical evaluation had been initiated, less than 10 per cent of the claimants had been assessed. When, therefore, in February 1989, the Supreme Court gave its blessing to the settlement between UOI and UCC, the compensation amount was not based on an assessment of all 600,000 claimants, nor on epidemiological evidence, but on totally mythical figures. The Supreme Court simply accepted a figure of 30,000 for those injured permanently and another 20,000 injured temporarily, based only on hospital records.

The Madhya Pradesh government presented its figures of numbers of injured, as assessed, in August 1989. According to them, of the total of 123,560 claimants, barely 800 were found to have permanent disability; extrapolating a figure in relation to the 600,000 claimants, would have meant that only 4,000 were to be considered permanently disabled. In October 1989, a critique by an independent group of researchers found that the gross under-estimation had resulted from faulty methodology which used arbitrary scores for assessing injury; claimed to identify disability in the absence of relevant information; did not carry out complete investigations; and relied on the production of records by the victims as proof of their exposure. By assessing a small sample population of the injured, using the diagnostic method followed in clinical practice, independent researchers could prove that more than 70-80 per cent of the gas-exposed population in the seriously affected municipal wards of Bhopal were permanently and seriously injured. This works out to approximately 300,000 to 400,000 victims suffering from serious medically diagnosable injury today.

In December 1989, with the change in national government, several groups representing the victims' interests came together to demand from the National Front government that interim relief be paid to the victims on the basis of residence on the night of December 2, 1984, and the consequent exposure to toxic gases. They also insisted that the personal injury evaluation followed by the Madhya Pradesh government should not form the basis for deciding the amount of interim relief. The government accepted this argument and decided to pay Rs 200 (USD 6.50) per month, per person, to all those resident in the 36 municipal wards of Bhopal who had been declared as directly exposed on the night of December 2, 1984. However, a major question still remained, i.e., on what basis was the settlement to be challenged? The National Front government announced that it proposed to support the efforts of the victims in re-opening the settlement; however, in court, its major emphasis was on the dropping of criminal charges against UCC. No effort was made to seriously question the level of compensation. But as a concession to the victims, the National Front government decided to relax the Official Secrets Act and released pertinent research findings of the ICMR and other research organisations to the victim groups.

From this information it became clear that the toxic gases had caused multi-systemic injury to those exposed to them. The damage caused was both irreversible, and led to progressive deterioration. Exposure had also damaged the immune system, so that previously asymptomatic persons were exhibiting symptoms at a later date. The possibility of later effects and unsuspected complications arising could not be ruled out, and there was a grave possibility of carcinogenic and mutagenic changes in the population.

While the information provided by the ICMR presented a serious scenario, the Madhya Pradesh government's estimate underplayed the nature and extent of injury. The court was confronted with two contradictory sets of information, both provided by government establishments: while that provided by the ICMR was on a small sample population, the Madhya Pradesh government claimed to have individually examined each claimant. In the absence of any scientifically valid assessment, one alternative was to identify the number of persons exposed in a given geographical area. The victims argued that all those exposed constituted an identifiable group that had been placed at increased risk. They argued further that the government had categorised the victims on the basis of an arbitrary scoring system, and that no effort had been made to diagnose and assess the injury and disability of each individual victim. Given the magnitude of the disaster and the nature of the injury, it was not reasonably possible to diagnose each and every victim or to assess the risk of future injury. Hence, the only rational method of arriving at an estimate of the number of persons injured would be to consider every exposed person as injured or potentially injured. This would be approximately 400,000. As against this, the figure agreed to by UOI and UCC had seemed absurdly low. Quite apart from the gross under-estimation of the number of persons injured, the actual amount agreed to be paid as compensation was unacceptable—ranging from Rs 10,000 to Rs 200,000 each (approximately USD 350–USD 6,500).

On October 3, 1991, the Supreme Court pronounced its judgment in the review petition: it held that the settlement was beyond challenge, that in the event of a shortfall in the compensation payable to the victims, the Government of India was liable to make good the shortfall, and that the criminal prosecution against UCC and UCIL (Union Carbide India, Ltd.) be dropped and its officials restored. The battle on behalf of the victims was already lost. The court refused to go into the question of the numbers of victims or the nature of the injury caused. As a result, the government's own estimates of the number of those injured has been accepted without question, leaving out of consideration the thousands of victims whose injuries remain unrecognised.

Bhopal: a global challenge

The extraordinary nature of this disaster and the unique circumstances of the litigation and judicial process over a period of seven years, raise some fundamental issues regarding rights jurisprudence itself, and the question of liability across international boundaries. It also compels us to reconsider the definition of compensation when long-term consequences are feared, and the scope of responsibility and liability when potentially hazardous substances are involved.

For Bhopal was not an isolated incident. A study of the Agent Orange Case reveals striking parallels. The Vietnam veterans who were exposed to Agent Orange, a herbicide used in the Vietnam war, had to accept a settlement very unfavourable to them, against their will and through a legal process. Medical information was suppressed and the medical community took refuge behind the near impossibility of doing a proper epidemiological study. If this is so, the intriguing question is: would the Bhopal settlement have been different if the case against UCC had been tried in the US? Perhaps not, because the political compulsions of the Indian government, which was the sole representative of the victims, would have been the same as the political compulsions exhibited by the American legal system in other disasters. Until today, the American transnational has not disclosed the chemical composition of the mixture of gases that leaked into the atmosphere in December 1984. When specifically asked to disclose these, they pleaded trade secrecy and took shelter behind patent laws.

In cases such as the Bhopal disaster, where the damage is latent and long-term, the invisible nature of the crime makes it possible for the court to evade the real issues because the law is so structured as to deal with the immediate and individual claim. In view of such cases, this may be an appropriate moment to look at the prevalent legal discourse on rights.

An analysis of the Bhopal case reveals that the origin of rights continues to spring from ownership of property rather than from a recognition of the needs of individuals. When the law looks at individuals it does so only in their capacity as political beings; hence, it confers political rights such as the right to freedom of speech, the right to vote, the right to form associations and so on. These rights inhere in individuals rather than in communities. It follows that there is no recognition of the right to protection of the environment, for such a right would by definition recognise collective control over common resources and a common heritage. For the first time, in 1986, motivated by the Bhopal disaster, the Government of India passed the Environment Protection Act which vests powers in the State to prevent the destruction of the environment, but unfortunately, even in this law, the conceptual framework of rights remains the same. The State continues to be both the enforcing agency, and the owner of all natural resources, so that the beneficiaries are still marginalised and have little or no role to play in the management and control of their own environment. The hallmark of all political formations after World War II is that the management and control of rights rests in the State. In a manner of speaking there is an unbroken link in the structure of legal control between colonial and post-colonial societies; only the managers of power have changed.

A significant function of the fact that ownership of property alone gives birth to rights, is that all rights are then capable of, and liable to, being monetised. What then is the measure of loss of rights? If one is measuring monetary loss, then the claim is reduced to the loss of earning capacity; thus a working-class man or woman would have lost his or her daily wage and will be compensated for that loss, whereas a businessman would lose his earning capacity, running probably into many millions, for which he will be compensated in millions. Unequal treatment is thus built into the structure of the law. The value of life is reduced to the value of its productive capacity measured in economic terms alone. Hence in the Bhopal case there is a total absence of a recognition of the violation of the right to dignity, the right to live in a healthy environment and the right to access to community resources. There is a corresponding absence of a recognition of the need to nurture and restore human life and ecosystems.

What rights for a sustainable society?

Any transitional rights jurisprudence would have to make a break with this concept of law and begin to talk of the right to restoration, to preservation, to creation, to community management and control over ecosystems. Such a discussion may also venture into areas such as whether rights must inhere in human beings alone or whether there is a value in recognising that they may inhere in the environment and in natural, depletable non-renewable resources, for and on their own behalf. In theory, rights to common resources such as forests, rivers, oceans and the earth itself are supposed to be vested in the State. By definition, therefore, rights are consequent upon power and the conferring of rights is organised into a system of licences given by the State, selectively. Individuals, on their own, have no role in the creation of rights or their enforcement; all they have is the right to manage their loss when it occurs.

The law has been unable to answer fundamental questions such as: who do the rivers belong to? who does the earth belong to? who does the environment belong to? and so on. All it has to say is that they belong to the legal fiction of the State. Thus, these natural resources which are vested in the State are then treated as capital and income-generating resources meant to be exploited for their commercial value. Having monopolised the ownership of natural resources, the State gives 'concessions', not rights, to individuals, and the nature of the discussion changes from one regarding rights to one dealing with concessions.

All recent movements that have to do with conserving the environment can be seen as an attempt to change the terms of the discourse from that of private rights vested in individuals, to public rights over common resources, vested in communities, and from individual ownership to collective control. These are movements which demand the freezing on further exploitation by the state of natural resources, and demand their inalienability. These movements represent a serious challenge to the structure and operation of law. The demand is for rights over life-support systems, not over rights to property and compensation. Any new rights jurisprudence would have to redefine the interrelationship between people and communities and the earth and its resources. The right to life-support systems would require an integrated approach towards the right to health and well-being, and the positive protection of what can be nurtured rather than negative relief through compensation.

When the State appropriates natural resources with their capacity to sustain life, it in effect appropriates the health and well-being of the people. The locating of a hazardous industry in a densely-populated community, simply because it owns the land and has the right to exploit it, has a direct bearing on the lives of members of that community. In the event of a disaster, the only 'right' that they then have is to try and contain it, to, in fact, 'manage' the disaster. They have no right to decide where hazardous industry should be located, only to claim compensation for the destruction of their right to life as a consequence of the former. This makes for a significant difference: while the rights to manage capital are determined and defined at the stage of production, the compensatory rights of victims are defined only at the point of destruction of life. Conceptually, the legal system has traditionally been incapable of anticipating rights.

Trade secrets and property rights

The mobility and convertability of resources are an essential prerequisite of trade and commerce, and they demand an equal degree of mobility and convertibility of rights. This latter is achieved by their monetisation: just as resources become transnational, so do rights become international and exportable. The mobility of capital brought with it the demand for mobility of rights. High on the agenda of transnationals today is the demand for the international protection of property rights, involving the necessary concomitant of secrecy in the technological, production and manufacturing processes. The issue which arose in the Bhopal disaster had largely to do with the protection of trade secrecy. The question of the 'autonomy' of technology has additional implications, especially regarding the health and well-being of peoples.

Given this propensity, we will be seeing more and more of transnational, rather than national, disasters. The practice of seeking remedies in national forums based on a plurality of laws is thus losing its relevance, and needs to be replaced by recourse to international forums with an international environmental and legal agenda, defined by a commonly binding set of standards and subject to an international regime of obligations towards people.

Shifts in the realm of rights would need to revolve around the relationship between people and their life-support systems, and the right of the community to decide on whether or not a hazardous industry should be allowed and where it should be located, whether or not a mine is dug or a river is dammed. These rights have to do with the very nature and structure of democracy, and when they are articulated from a people-centred perspective we will be moving in the direction of demanding the inalienability of natural and human resources, rather than their mobility and convertibility.

All the strongly held beliefs regarding the responsibilities of a socialist welfare State—transforming social relations, ensuring distribution of economic and social power, restricting monopolistic trade practices, etc.—have been called into question by the increasing privatisation of economies across the world and the yoking of all developing countries to a global market. This has resulted in a systematic dismantling of legislative control over economic activity, which means that, in essence, the legislative model is being reversed. The implications of this for rights jurisprudence need to be understood. The ostensible purpose of the exercise is to ensure the mobility of resources across national borders, with a corresponding mobility of rights across international borders. Hence, the insistent demand for changes in patent laws. It should be more than obvious, however, that the beneficiaries of this mobility of rights will be transnational corporations, for patents are a monetised form of rights. In a manner of speaking, transnationals then acquire the right to destroy, with no corresponding right in the community to stop such destruction. Any new rights jurisprudence, then, will have to ensure the right to creation and, equally, the right to prevent destruction.

'Green Earth, Women's Power, Human Liberation'

Women in Peasant Movements in India

Gail Omvedt

Introduction

When Columbus landed in America for the second time he brought with him stalks of sugarcane; sugar at that time was an extremely scarce and valuable item in the European diet. Planted in the West Indies and north-east Brazil, cane became the basis of the infamous 'triangular trade' linking the West Indies and New England, Britain and Africa in the production of sugar and rum, through the labour of slaves. It was also the beginning of ecologically destructive agriculture, for after flourishing for about a century in north-eastern Brazil sugar plantations rendered the land so unproductive that the region has remained the most impoverished in the country ever since.

Even before industrialism took hold, the rise of capitalism entailed the transformation of agriculture throughout the world. Some regions were turned into plantation colonies; in others, small peasants were forced through high taxes or other forms of bondage to produce crops for the European market; still others became sites of subsistence agriculture that functioned to reproduce the labour power of low-paid migrant workers in mines and factories. The forms varied, but there was a common thread. The extraction of surplus from the land, its forests, its plant and mineral wealth, was crucial to capital accumulation on a world scale. And it was accompanied by the exploitation, both direct and indirect,[1] of the women and men of peasant and forest-dwelling communities throughout the world. For any process of 'primitive accumulation' is, according to Marx, accompanied by violence, the 'midwife of history'.

When political independence came to nations in Africa and Asia, the ruling elite became the managers of the system of surplus accumulation and attempted to utilise it for development in their own societies. The main mechanisms for surplus extraction were by this time prices (low prices both for crops grown by peasant producers and for natural resources) and increasing state claims to ownership of common property which had once been under the control of village communities. Exploitation was masked by the ideology of development, in which the state proclaimed itself the driving force of industrialisation; low prices for peasant and forest products went along with 'state investment', with funds providing for agricultural inputs (such as fertiliser subsidies, large-scale irrigation projects, etc.) and 'schemes' for 'small and marginal farmers', women, the 'rural poor' or other victims of the development that was being fostered.

The results of this ecologically and humanly destructive system of agriculture have been widely documented. They have also awakened increasing resistance from the men and women of the communities, tribes, castes and nationalities that have been exploited and marginalised. The major force in this resistance has been the Third World peasantry, and the women of peasant communities have provided its core. Among the 'new social movements', which have developed in India during the last two decades,[2] two have been specifically rural: an environmental movement of peasants and tribals resisting drought, ecological destruction, displacement due to dams and other development projects; and the 'farmers' movement',[3] which has rallied peasants to fight their exploitation by the market and the state on issues such as prices, indebtedness, corruption. The first have been movements of the immediate victims of 'development'; the second have been movements of its supposed beneficiaries. Such movements began on more purely economic or survival issues, but by the late 1980s were putting forward various proposals for alternative development.

This contribution will focus on two organisations involved in these movements, both based in Maharashtra state of western India, and will examine in particular the role of rural women and the formation of an alternative developmental perspective. These organisations are *Mukti Sangharsh,* a movement of peasants and agricultural labourers fighting on issues of drought and water rights, and *Shetkari Sanghatana,* an organisation formed around the demand for fair prices for agricultural produce.

The characteristics of capitalist agriculture

First we should examine the major characteristics of the agricultural systems linked to capitalist-industrial development. Many people refer to 'commercial agriculture', but this term is not adequate: first, non-market state-controlled agriculture has been shown to be equally exploitative and ecologically destructive; second, the kind of agriculture or agro-industrial society it is contrasted with is not concerned only with pure subsistence production but involves some elements of trade, exchange and redistribution.

Ecologically and humanly destructive and exploitative agriculture, which has developed as part of the capitalist world system over the last five centuries, involves:

(1) *A high use of external inputs* brought over long distances by the state and transnational agencies, ranging from water provided through large-scale irrigation projects to manufactured items such as chemical fertilisers, pes-

ticides and hybrid seeds; this is in contrast to locally produced biologically-based inputs on which traditional systems rely.

(2) *A high degree of production for consumption elsewhere*, often a long distance away, of food crops such as grain, fruit and vegetables, raw materials such as cotton and extracted products such as fish and forest products. This is in contrast with the traditional pattern of mainly local consumption with long-distance trade only in luxuries.

(3) *The predominance of monoculture*, in contrast to diversified cropping patterns.

(4) *Uneven development,* characterised by islands of seeming prosperity contrasted with 'backward', drought-prone regions. Pre-colonial agriculture in countries such as India included a wide variety of local production systems appropriate to a diverse ecology. The types of agriculture practised in forest, grassland or dry regions and the 'wet' agriculture of delta or river valley areas very often coexisted as mutually supportive systems of production. Capitalist agriculture erases such distinctions and, in its homogenising sweep, tends to promote similar kinds of cultivation everywhere; dry-land agriculture simply becomes a less successful version of irrigated agriculture, while at the same time the natural sources of agricultural inputs for the more highly productive crop regions are destroyed.[4]

(5) *The encroachment on local decision-making power and local control of production processes* by national and international forces; research and innovation become the property of capitalist forces claiming the sanctity of science, and local toilers, men and women, become only receivers of information. This contrasts with traditional patterns of local innovation and pre-colonial systems where women normally had a substantial role in decision-making and in control of production.

(6) *The intensification of local inequalities*. This does not usually take the form that traditional Marxist theory predicted: a transformation of the peasant community into a polarised arrangement of classes in which agricultural labourers confront capitalist farmers. Instead, alongside plantation economies, peasant producers who still have access to land are transformed into labourers producing for capital and the state via control over their inputs and the marketing of produce. Traditional hierarchies in countries such as India (involving caste and gender interacting with uneven access to economic resources such as control of land) survive, though their forms may change; and traditional landlords are replaced by capitalist farmers, but without a significant increase in absolute land concentration or landlessness.[5] The rural oligarchy or power elite, which operates in sometimes brutal and sometimes sophisticated fashion, is less and less a class of traditional landlords or a simple accumulating bourgeoisie, and consists more and more of link men with access to the larger system: political bosses, contractors, smugglers, agents for fertiliser companies, whose wealth and

power, while connected with agriculture, have their most important base outside it.

(7) *Exploitation in the specifically Marxist sense as well as damage to ecology and human health*. While environmentalists have tended to speak of destruction and to overlook exploitation, Marxists have ignored the exploitation involved in non-wage labour production. It is now clear, however, that the Indian economy in recent decades has been characterised not by inequalities within agriculture but by a growing gap between the organised and unorganised sectors (the latter including peasant cultivators and agricultural labourers as well as non-agricultural wage workers and self-employed) and that agricultural incomes are at the bottom of the economic scale.[6] This depression of the agricultural sector as a whole is another characteristic of the system.

Peasant resistance movements

The final characteristic of capitalist agriculture is perhaps that it would like to abolish the peasants or farmers themselves: to create either a totally mechanised agriculture with no human producers, or to turn peasants into labourers on large-scale farms, carrying out tasks totally set from above, with no more relation to the land than factory workers have to raw materials. The subordination of petty commodity producers to capital and the state, through control of their markets and the provision of inputs which essentially determine the production process, represents a step along this line of development. But, unlike industry, the nature of the land and of food production probably makes full control next to impossible. Peasants and peasant communities, such as forest-dwelling communities, have stubbornly refused to vanish, resisting their exploitation, the appropriation of their resources and the destruction of their conditions of production. This resistance has been a major factor in social history this century, and both the environmental movement and the farmers' movement have become a significant force in India today.

Environmental movements have been locally organised, usually covering a group of villages where people are affected by harmful 'development'; farmers' movements are large popular movements covering many districts of a state and mobilising in hundreds of thousands for major campaigns and rallies. For example, Mukti Sangharsh covers many of the 108 villages in Sangli district in Maharashtra, while Shetkari Sanghatana is a force in perhaps half of the districts of the state. Aside from the difference in scope, the movements have many characteristics in common. They are not NGOs or funded agencies; they are mass-based, self-financed people's movements (to take a simple criterion, they are not registered, though associated registered organisations may provide facilitating services). They have formal structures of varying degrees, but informal structures and spontaneity play a major role in their operation. This is particularly important with regard to women, who are often more involved at the informal level and unrepresented or under-represented in formal decision-making structures. Their agitations tend to be directed against the state, or sometimes large corporations, the forces behind displacement, land take-overs etc., rather than against local big landlords or moneylenders. They are non-party (not officially connected with any political party) and frequently hostile to all parties for not dealing with their problems. While in India, at least, they have identified with oppositional left and democratic politics, this has always been in tension with the parties claiming to stand for such politics.

Both types of movements are 'all-peasants' movements, though many organisers operate with some notion of divisions among the peasantry, seeking to promote the interests of the poor and sideline the richer farmers in some way. The farmers' movements criticise all rich peasant/poor peasant divisions as tending to weaken peasant resistance. They often define their movement to include people in occupations associated with agriculture (artisans, small traders, agricultural labourers as well as land-owning peasants), either broadening the definition of 'peasant' or (like the Ryot Sangh in Karnataka) saying, 'we are not a peasant movement but a village movement'. But environmental movements also include a wide variety of producers in the affected areas (for example, Balliapal with its fishermen, rich farmers and labourers) and are sometimes criticised by leftists for this reason.

Finally, there are a number of ironies about the way in which the movements are seen by the bureaucracy and bourgeoisie. There is invariably repression and opposition, but the ideological forms in which the spokesmen of capitalist interests deal with the movements are different. The farmers' movements are stamped as 'kulak', and those behind them seen as 'rich peasants' representing rural ruling interests. Environmentalism, in contrast, is romanticised while its goals are distorted. Activists seen as working on behalf of 'victimised tribals' may be praised, while the state continues to put itself forward as the only force capable of carrying out real reforms. In both cases ideological and political attacks attempt to show the movements as being against other sections of the poor and exploited: peasant demands for higher crop prices are attacked for making food expensive for the poor, while environmentalism is criticised as 'standing in the way of development'.

Mukti Sangharsh and Stri Mukti Sangharsh

Sangli district in southern Maharashtra is considered one of the developed regions of the state, but it is only the valley of the Krishna river that is the irrigated, sugarcane-producing heart of the region. Most of the district is dry and drought-prone. The whole area has a history of anti-caste democratic and nationalist struggles. Mukti Sangharsh (the name means Liberation Struggle, and is the short form of Exploited Peasants, Workers and Toilers' Liberation Struggle) was formed in one of these dry areas, Khanapur, after the massive Bombay textile strike of 1982-83 when workers from the area returned to their villages and began to organise, first around their own demands and then in support of building a peasant movement.

Drought was the overriding reality of the region and the period, and from the beginning Mukti Sangharsh had a new perspective on the issue. Whereas almost all organisations, whether NGOs or party-connected mass organisations, have spoken of 'alleviating drought', demanding relief schemes and especially the work projects (EGS or employment guarantee schemes) provided by the state government, Mukti Sangharsh took as its aim *eradicating drought*. Its major slogan was, 'we won't break rocks, we won't lay roads, we won't stop without eradicating drought', and this became particularly popular with the women involved in struggle, who carried it with them into participation in united women's activities.

What 'eradicating drought' required was not immediately clear, and a period of research and experiment began. Activists and peasants toured Khanapur, surveying wells and rivers, and brought out a booklet giving their results and making suggestions that began to propose locally-based alternatives such as percolation tanks. A 'people's science march' was held. In 1985 a drought eradication conference was organised, which included discussions with experts and labour organisers on means of distributing water more widely and equitably. Just before the conference a peasants' march on the university had been staged. Five hundred peasants came to the university gates, demanding that either professors do drought-connected research and translate it into their language, or they themselves would go into the library and do the work. They were met at the time by police, but the action ultimately resulted in a fruitful collaboration with university officials and some professors and students.

The most famous struggle of Mukti Sangharsh began in 1986 and centred on the efforts of peasants to build a small dam, the Bali Raja Memorial Dam, irrigating 900 acres in two villages. Its functioning included the principle that water would be provided on an equal basis to all, even the landless (who could sell their water shares, lease in land, or whatever), making it generally impossible to monopolise water for high water-using crops such as sugarcane. The major conflict was not with local rich farmers, but with the state bureaucracy, and it revolved round the question of sand. Like other natural resources in India, sand is considered the property of the state and not the village community; it was being extracted from the bed of the Yerala River running between the villages (a river which dried up for 11 months of the year), making huge profits for both contractors and many in the bureaucracy. The peasants simply demanded the right to use the sand in their area to finance the dam, serving the interests of eradicating drought rather than profiting from it, adding that they could do this in a non-damaging way while the contractors' 'mining' of the sand had a destructive effect on the percolation of the water. It was this underlying economic interest—surplus extracted in the form of sand—that resulted in even a very small dam being an issue that had to be fought for five years, with marches, demonstrations, road blocks by humans and bullocks, the rallying of a united front comprising representatives of all opposition parties, and a movement going up to the level of the state government itself, before the peasants won the right to build their own dam.

More recently, Mukti Sangharsh has been confronting the bureaucracy over the Takari scheme, a lift-irrigation project costing Rs 5 billion which proposes to lift water from the Krishna River to irrigate the drought-prone areas of the district. But for Khanapur, rather than meeting the needs of all drought-stricken villages, the scheme was designed to irrigate only eight villages fully and 22 partially, again creating islands of development in a drought-prone sea. Mukti Sangharsh activists drew up an alternative plan, based on their experience in the Bali Raja dam struggle and drawing on various experiments in biomass-based sustainable agriculture. They showed that the same amount of water could be used to give all families in 60 villages enough water to irrigate three acres, meeting minimum needs of food grain, fodder, fuel, vegetables and fruit trees which could provide cash. With 60 villages using the Krishna in this way, the remaining villages could, it was estimated, get sufficient water from local rainfall and from minor irrigation projects to protect the whole area from the ravages of drought. Campaigns are now underway linking the issue of dams and irrigation with alternative forms of equitable and sustainable agricultural production.

Women have been enthusiastic participants in these struggles, particularly for the Bali Raja dam, though as elsewhere they have little role in decision-making. In 1985 they formed their own organisation, *Stri Mukti Sangharsh Calval* (Women's Liberation Struggle Movement). In part this emerged from the Khanapur-based movement, in part from links with other areas in the region. Thus as it spread, it began to attain a real autonomy from Mukti Sangharsh, though as with all rural women's organisations the cooperation of male activists was indispensible. Initial organising issues centred around those of employment in the EGS schemes, fighting atrocities, and general consciousness-raising.

Then in 1987 a new campaign was taken up when Stri Mukti Sangharsh began to organise 'abandoned women', those divorced or deserted by their husbands. The numbers of such women from all castes and religious communities are increasing in the villages; they are normally sent back to their parental villages where they have to support themselves and their children by working as labourers without rights in either the house or land of their natal family. Their situation reflects the social condition of women within the Hindu patriarchal family system, as essentially landless, homeless and without support.

Along with this, Stri Mukti Sangharsh has been part of a broad platform of progressive women's organisations in the state. It joined the campaign led by Shetkari Sanghatana women to organise 'all-women panels' for district council elections (in fact, women connected with Stri Mukti Sangharsh organised one of the first, though unsuccessful, efforts by women to contest village elections in 1985). It has developed close relations with the National Federation of Indian Women (NFIW), the women's organisation linked to the Communist Party of India. Members have also been active in anti-caste and anti-communal campaigns.

Gradually an ecological perspective has been growing in the organisation as a whole, and from 1990 a new slogan, *hirvi dharti, stri shakti, manav mukti* (green earth, women's power, human liberation) began to be used. Stri Mukti Sangharsh activists are now working with a Bombay-based organisation of engineers and scientists in projects aimed at making rural women a core part of the development of alternative technology and alternative agriculture; they are beginning in the area of Bali Raja dam with nursery development and with vegetable plots for women. At a camp, held in August 1991, on 'women and agriculture', representatives of some 25 villages, including both agricultural labourers and peasant women, compared their experiences of the generally greater women's role in decision-making in traditional, biomass-based agriculture with their exclusion from this in contemporary 'green revolution' agriculture. There was also a discussion of women's land rights and the possibilities of women gaining access to land, either some share in family land or control over government-held waste lands as part of a programme of biomass-based production. After a long struggle with local officials, 24 abandoned women in one village have finally had their claim to plots for houses recognised; individual women elsewhere have been included in programmes to allocate plots to women, and one local women's organisation connected with Mukti Sangharsh is proposing taking out a lease on the 100 acres of 'waste land' near their village.

Shetkari Sanghatana and Shetkari Mahila Aghadi

At the other end of the spectrum, apparently, from localy based movements like Mukti Sangharsh which have focused directly on creating alternatives, is Shetkari Sanghatana (Peasants' Organisation) with its market-oriented demand of fair prices and its charismatic leader Sharad Joshi (a retired official of the Universal Postal Union) arguing that this 'one-point programme' was sufficient to reverse the course of destructive development. Not only have leftists and bourgeois intellectuals stamped the movement as 'kulak';

but most environmentalists have also seen it as having a purely market orientation of little interest to those concerned with alternatives.

Yet, just as the peasants and forest-dwellers victimised by developmental projects start with survival issues and only gradually move on to questioning the whole model of development, for peasants drawn into market production in general, the question of alternatives has also arisen out of issues of immediate economic exploitation. The Shetkari Sanghatana's slogan, 'We don't want alms, but the return for our sweat', illustrates the sense of a struggle against exploitation. At the same time, the search for better terms on the market has nearly always been accompanied by an awareness of the problems of the new capitalist agriculture. Peasants have a fundamental ambivalence towards the agricultural system which gives them immediate profits but often renders them indebted and impoverished in unforeseen ways in the long run.

Almost all the various new farmers' organisations in India have some element of Gandhian ideology and look towards a village-centred, decentralised type of development. The very forms of struggle of the movement have been those of delinking from state and market: *rasta raka* or roadblocking, cutting the links between city and villages, and *gavbardi,* in which officials and political leaders are declared barred from the villages. Behind Shetkari Sanghatana's one-point programme lies in fact an ideology stressing that if surplus is left in the hands of the peasants, they themselves would create a more sustainable, village-based, agro-industrial development. In the world of Sunil Saharsabudhe:

An important feature of the peasant movement is that none of its demands are for development in the rural areas. They have neither asked for easier terms of credit nor for opening of schools and hospitals. In fact, the movement presents an entirely new concept of development.... When the peasant gets the extra money, which is his due, he will invest it in the manner he deems fit. It will be up to him to decide whether to build roads and canals, establish schools and hospitals, develop research laboratories, carry out research on the farm or do whatever else he may think necessary and useful.... Eradication of the poverty of the rural people, not through development, but by giving them fair returns for their produce, is the strongest and most radical argument for decentralisation.... The peasant movement is thus committed to eradicate the poverty of the rural people by undoing 'development' in theory and in practice.[7]

Shetkari Sanghatana itself moved away from its one-point programme when it took up women's issues in 1986 and made it clear that women's oppression would not necessarily be ended even if peasants won their price demands. Before this, however, came the movement's 1984-85 crisis over the encircling of the assembly building at Chandigarh, the threatened boycott of wheat from the Punjab, and Operation Bluestar, a sequence described by

Vandana Shiva in *Violence of the Green Revolution*.[8] The events highlighted
the interweaving of the tensions linked to chemical-industrial agriculture
and the national political crisis, and were preceded by the Shetkari
Sanghatana's 1984 session at Parbhani, which had threatened an overall
boycott of industrial inputs as well as production for home consumption
only, as a major part of the fight against the state.

The organisation of a massive women's conference of the Shetkari
Sanghatana in 1986 represented both a recovery from a period of lull for the
movement and a striking out in new directions. With nearly two hundred
thousand peasant women and men in attendance, proclaiming the slogan
Stri Shakticya Jagranat Stri-Purush Mukti (Liberation of Women and Men in
the Awakening of Women's Power), it saw resolutions on women's property
rights, education, drought, a common civil code, and the establishment of
a women's front, the *Shetkari Mahila Aghadi* (Peasant Women's Alliance).
Its boldest call was a challenge to women to monopolise political power: district council elections were soon to be held in the state, and the conference
called for women's organisations to come together to form all-women
panels to fight the elections; political parties, especially those on the democratic left, were asked to provide support. 'Peasants cannot become a
national political force', declared Sharad Joshi at the conference, 'but
women can be'.

At the same time, women began to go ahead on their own locally. Village
council elections were held in 1989-90 in Maharashtra state and peasants in
several villages influenced by Shetkari Sanghatana independently put up
all-women panels, although this was not an overall Sanghatana programme
at the village level. Seven of these were elected, among the first all-women
village councils in India. At the same time, campaigns against alcoholism
were initiated, and another major aspect of women's subordinated position,
their effective exclusion from ownership of land and other property in spite
of laws granting inheritance and property rights, became increasingly a matter of discussion and action.

Is women's empowerment connected with other aspects of social transformation? The significance of raising the political question for women can
be seen in the nature of the manifesto adopted by the Samagra Mahila
Aghadi for district council elections. Though the major force behind this
was Shetkari Sanghatana, the manifesto did not mention price or market
issues at all, but rather concentrated on outlining a women-oriented alternative develoment:

Through taking in hand panchayat raj women's participation in public life will increase ... the direction of development will be seen from a women's perspective.
Priority will be given to such programmes as women's health, nutrition, drinking
water facilities and cleanliness. Today we see only the ferocious dance of corruption

and self-interest. These will be checked and real programmes of development will be taken up.[9]

In other words, it was through the involvement of women that notions of alternative development, which had been only implicit in earlier peasant struggles, began to be placed directly on the agenda. Such programmes have begun to be implemented in the villages with all-women village councils.

Early in 1990, men and women of Vitner, a small village on the banks of the Tapi river in Jalgaon district and one of the five with an all-women council, took a big step forward in giving women the legal rights to a share of the family property. This became a fully fledged campaign for Shetkari Sanghatana and its women's front, under the slogan *Lasmi Mukti* (Liberate the Goddess of Wealth). By the middle of 1991 over 100 peasant families in each of nearly 300 villages had given land rights to women, a significant move in combating the powerless and resourceless position of Indian women.

At the same time, 1991 developments were making for an entirely new environment for the farmers' movement. Fertiliser subsidies have been a linchpin of Green Revolution technology in the countries of the South. In the context of the IMF loan, the new India budget had proposed a drastic reduction in fertiliser subsidies. From Shetkari Sanghatana's viewpoint, subsidies were only another trick on the part of a government that fostered an inefficient state-run fertiliser industry rather than giving farmers remunerative prices; moreover, the National Agricultural Policy had been opposed to subsidies. But the habit of seeing subsidies as a state programme benefiting peasants and crucial to growth in agricultural production had died hard. Peasants themselves throughout India were ambivalent about the issue, but politicians were not: Janata Dal factions, many Congress leaders, and the established left parties leapt into the fray, organising peasant demonstrations and demanding a full restoration of subsidies.

Yet, even here a search for alternatives could be seen. The Shetkari Sanghatana leadership, while welcoming the new weakness of the central state (shown by the fact that it no longer had the capacity to hold down crop prices), announced a new programme at a massive, 3-400,000-strong rally in the small town of Shegaon on November 10, 1991. Peasants, declared Sharad Joshi, were now to fight the battle of production. Up to now, state control and 'expert advice' had kept prices low, below the world market level; now 'liberalisation' meant that the state was too weak to keep the peasant in bondage any longer. Peasants were now free to produce, but it was to be a self-determined production. A programme of 'four-sided agriculture' was given, to include (i) agriculture for export: India has a comparative advantage in primary produce; peasants could thus 'save the nation through foreign exchange earnings'; (ii) commercial agriculture, or the effort to establish direct consumer-producer linkages; (iii) agriculture-with-processing; and (iv) *Sita Sheti* or 'Sita agriculture', i.e. farming on small plots (often the land put in women's names), which was to be experimental, low-input farming primarily to serve the household's needs for food.

All these varied forms of agricultural production (and agro-processing) were to be done with only a minimal use of expensive chemical-industrial external inputs, i.e. exporting was to be done without import-dependence and aimed at health-food markets; processing was to be small-scale and removed from mechanical factory production. 'Sita agriculture', in particular, was essential to the shift to sustainability. It was to be consciously experimental, without incurring expense, to use water available locally and to rely on soil creation (composting). In the first training session, S.Y. Dabholkar, a widely known experimental agriculturalist from southern Maharashtra, proclaimed the leading role of the women's front in moving towards energy-recycling, regenerative agricultural production.

As yet, the 'Sita sheti' programme is in its early phase. Male activists appear to view it as a leading force in a shift to low-input agriculture. Large numbers of farming families who find it impractical suddenly to drop all chemical-industrial inputs are quite ready to give over a plot of land for experimentation. As for the women themselves, the degree to which it becomes a means to recover their former central role in agricultural decision-making and production will be one of the interesting questions for the next decade of Shetkari Sanghatana's activity. Only a few have begun to reclaim their rightful position, though these include some assertive women activists taking on a major role in family agriculture; but many more are putting new processing ideas into practice and looking to develop local markets for them.

Towards Alternative Development

By the 1990s calls for 'alternative development' or 'people's development' were being made more and more often, emanating in particular from environmental movements, including local struggles over water distribution, such as that organised by Mukti Sangharsh. At the same time, many sections of the farmers' movement, much larger and hitherto more politically effective, were becoming concerned not simply with winning better terms within the market system of capitalist agriculture, but with a search for alternatives to this system. In view of the marginalisation and super-exploitation of women's labour linked to the system, it is perhaps not surprising that women seeking their own empowerment should become forces supporting a new kind of development. In this, science and technology were to be participatory, and applied to decentralised, biomass-based village production systems. In the turmoil and confusion characterising Indian and world politics in the 1990s, these developments concerning the role of women in peasant movements were showing a shift of potentially great significance.

Notes

1. We might speak of 'indirect exploitation' when capitalist expansion destroys the conditions of production or livelihood for otherwise isolated communities, forcing them to work harder to survive as before.
2. See my *Reinventing Revolution: India's New Social Movements*, M.E. Sharpe Inc., New York, (forthcoming), for a fuller account of these movements.
3. Although a 'farmer' generally produces for the market while a 'peasant' is involved in subsistence production, Indian languages do not distinguish between the two terms, and most Indian peasants/farmers are mixed producers, consuming much of their own produce but generally engaged in some market relations.
4. There is a tendency to see cultivators in the irrigated islands of development, such as Punjab and the northwest of India, as favoured in contrast to impoverished dry-land peasants; just as people sometimes see peasants benefiting from dams and irrigation as sharing in the exploitation of those displaced. It is important to note that the system itself sets up these contradictions—for instance, all dams create immediate conflicts of interest between the command area and the catchment area. In fact, only different forms of exploitation and surplus extraction are created. The 'islands of development' are themselves implied by the system: the need to feed concentrated areas of non-food producing working classes implies the need to establish other areas of reliable food production.
5. Gini coefficient ratios have slightly dropped overall since independence, showing a decline after land reforms, then a growth between 1961-62 and 1971-72, then a decline in 1981-82; the proportion of rural households cultivating no land rose from 10.96 per cent in 1953-54 to 27.41 per cent in 1971-72 (though only 9 per cent owned no land) and then dropped again to 23.7 per cent in 1981-82. The percentage of agricultural labourers has been rising (though census statistics on this issue have to be read in the light of a significant under-counting of peasant cultivators due to inadequate recognition of women's labour), but most of these have been labourers with small plots of land, i.e. marginalised peasants rather than true 'proletarians', and the overall picture has been one of a 'pushing down' of the entire rural class structure without increasing differentiation; small peasants with marginalised holdings have maintained their share in the community. See the National Sample Surveys, especially the All-India Debt and Investment Survey, *Assets of Rural Households as on 30 June, 1971*, Reserve Bank of India, Bombay, 1976, p. 39, Table 2.5, All-India Debt and Investment Survey, *Assets of Rural and Urban Households as on 30 June 1981*, Reserve Bank of India, Bombay, p. 5, and Kristnaji, N., 'Land and Labour in India: The Demographic Factor', *Economic and Political Weekly*, May 5-12, 1990.
6. For instance, the share in national income of the organised sector, comprising about 10 per cent of all the working population, rose from 23.6 per cent in 1960-61 to 37.8 per cent in 1984-85, according to the Centre for Monitoring the Indian

Economy, *Basic Statistics on the Indian Economy: Volume I, All-India*, Bombay, 1987, Table 8.5-B; while in 1981, the incomes of organised sector workers averaged about Rs 10,000, those of unorganised sector non-agricultural self-employed Rs 5,000, of non-agricultural wage workers Rs 4,800, of cultivating peasants Rs 3,000, and of agricultural labourers Rs 1,700 (ibid., Table 10.1). In other words, while agricultural labourers were clearly the poorest, landholding peasants (and only a small percentage of land was under tenancy in India by this time) had average incomes significantly below even unorganised sector wage workers. A working paper for a seminar of left economists in February 1991 linked the growing shares of national income held by organised sector workers, especially public sector employees, to the economic crisis that led up to the IMF loan; see 'From Loan to Loan', *Frontline,* March 16-29, 1991.

7. Saharashbudhe, Sunil, 'Peasant Movement and the Question of Development', in Karna, M.N. (ed.), *Peasants and Peasant Protest in India*, Intellectual Publishing House, New Delhi, 1985, p. 152.
8. Shiva, Vandana, *Violence of the Green Revolution*, Third World Network, 1991, see also Roosa, John, 'The Punjab Crisis; Fallout of the Green Revolution', September 1989 (unpublished manuscript).
9. Samagra Mahila Aghadi manifesto, adopted July 1987.

Filipino Peasant Women in Defence of Life

Loreta B. Ayupan and Teresita G. Oliveros

Struggles to sustain life

Aling Masang, a widowed peasant woman from Langkaan, Dasmarinas, Cavite, walked about uneasily in her small nipa hut. The early morning rays of the sun had just begun to spread. She tried to relax, taking deep breaths as she surveyed the land and the environment outside her hut. A few metres away ran the river, clear and still unpolluted, a source of water for washing and other household needs. The river, which had borne witness to all their life struggles, would now perhaps see their eviction from this piece of land that she, her parents, and their ancestors had cleared and nurtured. By some twist of fate, and due to their ignorance and lack of education, title to the land was in the name of another family who, they heard, were planning to either sell or develop the land into a sub-division or an industrial estate to capitalise on the development targeted for Cavite.

Later in the morning, Aling Masang together with the women in the barrio—pregnant women, nursing mothers, old women and children—lined up to form a human barricade across the road. Armed with *bolos* and stones, the women and children confronted the evacuation team, their tractors and their heavily armed guards. Aling Masang led the negotiations and was successful in stopping the team from starting up their tractors to clear the land for sugarcane planting. The women determinedly declared: 'We are not afraid of your guns! We are not afraid to die! Dying from your bullets is instant death. Losing our land is slow death for us, as it will bring about famine and hunger and the death of our rivers and everything alive in this land!'

The team, which included military men, turned and left. This victory, albeit temporary, further strengthened the resolve of the women to continue fighting. People on the other side of barrio Langkaan had already been displaced by the Marubeni Corporation, a Japanese firm that was building an industrial estate in the area. The farmers were only paid what they called 'disturbance compensation'.

The Marubeni Industrial Estate is only one of the projects under the Calabarzon development of the Philippine government. Calabarzon is an acronym of Cavite, Laguna, Batangas, Rizal and Quezon, the five provinces in southern Luzon, adjacent to Metro Manila, whose development as an industrial zone, where foreign investors could establish factories and industries, was begun by the Aquino government. Aling Masang and her barrio-mates are still in Langkaan, but they do not know how long they can hold on. They have only their unity as a weapon.

Meanwhile, in barrio Tartaria in the adjacent town of Silang, peasant women of the UGIT organisation affiliated to AMIHAN, the Peasant Women's Federation, blocked and drove away a team of surveyors ordered to survey the area where there was a proposal to build a market, slaughterhouse and cemetery to service the needs of the future population, attracted to the area by the Calabarzon project. Led by Teresita Alvarez, the women expressed their disagreement with the plan, claiming that pollution of the river systems and soil destruction would be the inevitable result. Faced with their resistance, the survey team backed off and left.

A day after the incident, the women called for a barrio meeting to hold a dialogue with the barangay captain and drew up their unified position against the plan. The barangay captain promised only to inform the governor of their opposition. Although the threat of displacement still exists, the women and the barrio residents are more determined now to organise and defend their land from being converted to other uses, leaving them and their families vulnerable to hunger.

These are only two of the countless stories of peasant women in the Philippines who are struggling to sustain and defend life by being prepared to sacrifice their own. For peasant women in the Philippines, the survival of their families and communities is synonymous with the survival and preservation of the environment.

The reasons are not hard to find. Seventy per cent of the population of the Philippines depends on the country's natural resources for its livelihood. Almost half the country's total land area of 30 million hectares is suitable for agricultural cultivation. The Bureau of Agricultural Statistics (BAS) estimated in 1989 that 13.1 million hectares, or 44 per cent of the land, was utilised for agricultural production; another 1.6 million hectares were either under-utilised or idle. According to a study by the National Council for Integrated National Development, the resources of the country could provide food for 126 million people—double the current population.

However, the development model that the Philippine government follows is based on the dictates of the powerful international capitalist bloc. The Philippines is a neo-colonial economy, dependent on selling its produce in the world market in order to finance development and pay back its gigantic foreign debt. For more than two decades now, it has been wedded to export-led production. The utilisation of land resources is based on the nutritional and commercial value of crops planted. While food crops cater to the sustenance needs of the local population, cash crops fulfil the foreign exchange needs of the country. The area devoted to food crops is still larger than that under cash-crop cultivation. According to the National Statistics Office, the percentage share of land devoted to food crops in 1989 was 63.2 per cent compared to 36.8 per cent for cash crops. The main cash crops are coconut, sugarcane, banana and pineapple. Among the food crops, rice and corn, the staple food of the Filipinos, are the most important.

A bitter irony for the agricultural sector is that while the country experienced a boom in rice production in the 1960s and 1970s, the Green Revolution programme, from the late 1970s to the present, has seen chronic rice and corn shortages which have jacked up the prices of these commodities. From the 1980s to the present, the Philippines has overtaken Hawaii as the world's largest pineapple exporter, and now controls 90 per cent of the Japanese market for bananas. And yet, the people remain poor and hungry.

Where then does the root of the problem lie?

Two major government projects will be presented here as a starting point for understanding the economy of the country, the destructive effect of government policies on our natural resources and environment, and on agriculture's productive forces—peasant men and peasant women—whose labour ensures the survival of the country.

The Calabarzon project

The Calabarzon project is only one of the development projects of the Philippine government under the Philippine Assistance Program (PAP), and is seen as a model for similar projects planned for other regions in the country. The 3,000-hectare Phividec Industrial Estate in Mindanao is to be expanded; to be constructed across the country are the General Santos Agro-Industrial Project in Mindanao; the Samar Island Development Project and the Panay-Negros Agro-Industrial project in the Visayas, among others. As conceived, Calabarzon will make the five provinces of southern Tagalog an extension of Metro Manila. It will transform the fertile agricultural lands of southern Tagalog into industrial sites which will then be opened up to foreign capital. Components of the programme for the development of the area are: the expansion of the Batangas City seaport, funded by Japan's Overseas Economic Cooperation Fund (OECF), the construction designed and managed by the Japanese International Cooperation Agency (JICA); and the establishment of a telecommunications system, to be funded by a loan from the OECF.

In the Calabarzon plan, the country will continue to build industrial estates, which are really export-processing zones. An international port is to be constructed at Infanta, Quezon, which faces the Pacific Ocean, creating an accessible route to Japan and the United States, the country's top export markets. Electrical services will be expanded by building power generation plants, and road works and communication networks will be added. Almost all these projects are funded by the OECF, with support from the World Bank and from Germany's Kreditanstalt für Wiederaufbau.

But the people have no reason to rejoice. The construction of industrial estates has consistently resulted in the displacement of thousands of poor farming families, as happened when the country's four export-processing zones were set up. Peasant families are further victimised in a country with an unresolved and highly destabilising problem of landlessness. The construction of industrial estates on what used to be prime agricultural land pushes displaced peasants on to upland areas, whose exploitation in turn threatens biodiversity and soil fertility. With no support structures and mechanisms for agricultural production, upland dwellers are sometimes forced to engage in illegal logging activities just so that they can provide for their families.

The Calabarzon project includes lowlands, uplands and coastal zones, magnifying the danger of social and economic displacement within the project area. When fully completed, the project will have displaced an estimated 100,000 peasant families, according to the non-governmental Coalition of Organisations for Solidarity Tourism. Because the areas covered by Calabarzon are noted for supplying Metro Manila and adjacent areas with migrant labour, we can even safely assume that a good number of these displaced families may be female-headed.

There may not even be any compensation at all for the displaced. The project may not employ the people in the area, and some critics have pointed out that the government can only promise some 340,000 new jobs, whereas a much bigger number of people are likely to be displaced. As Aling Masang has said, 'How can we work in the factories when capitalists demand that their workers should have finished high school?' A good percentage of Filipinos have not even completed elementary school; in fact, a recently conducted study by the Department of Education, Culture and Sports revealed that there are more than 2.6 million illiterates in the 15-54 year-old age group in the rural areas.

At issue is the government's concept of industrialisation. The country's abundant raw materials and cheap labour have always been utilised to produce goods for consumption in the North. Incentives to prospective investors, almost always foreign, include the unrestricted repatriation of profits, tax holidays, and the availability of local capital to make up their limited capital investment.

Filipino peasants view this as no less than a sell-out of the country to profit-hungry transnational corporations, an opening of the floodgates to foreign exploitation and the plunder of our natural resources, and environmental degradation. Because these projects do not cater to the local market, foreign investors cannot be expected to be sensitive to Filipino demands to produce only what is socially necessary and ensure that production does not threaten the health and welfare of workers and consumers, nor the ecological balance on which farm production is dependent.

To the detriment of Filipinos, especially the women who are losing their hold on the land, landlords refused to sell their land according to the requirements of the Comprehensive Agrarian Reform Law (CARL). A massive conversion of agricultural land to industrial uses is now being undertaken by the landlords, so much so that even those who had offered to sell their land to the government on a voluntary offer to sell (VOS) scheme are now reneging on their pledges and applying for conversion of their agricultural holdings to industrial land use.

A very alarming implication of this is the environmental degradation that would ensue as a result. Many of the corporations that are expected to set up their plants in the country have been rejected in their own countries because of pollution hazards. An example of this is the Luzon Petrochemical Complex which will be set up in Batangas: it was rejected in its home country, Taiwan, because of the enormous pollution that petrochemical processing entails. Another case is the Kawasaki Sintering Plant, set up in the southern province of Misamis Oriental in the mid-1970s amid noisy protest, both in the Philippines and Japan, over the pollution inherent in the sintering process. This project displaced about 300 peasant families in an area contiguous to the expanding Phividec Industrial Estate.

With the Calabarzon project, the whole ecological make-up of the five provinces of southern Luzon is being altered. Laguna Lake, a rich fishing ground and a source of livelihood for thousands of fisherfolk, is being tapped as a primary power source, in addition to what is already generated by the hydroelectric plants surrounding it. A treatment plant reservoir, pumping stations and aqueduct system will soon siphon off the waters of Laguna Lake to provide the water needed by Calabarzon and Metro Manila. Government plans indicate that 85 per cent of the lake's waters will be used for this purpose, and only 12 per cent for irrigation, and three per cent for fisheries. This plan will displace 400,000 Filipinos who live off agriculture and aquaculture in the lake area, while only a maximum of 340,000 Filipinos will benefit directly.

To generate electrical power for the factories, the Calaca geothermal plant is being expanded in Batangas; the consequent increase in emission of sulphuric fumes can only aggravate existing pollution levels.

Another alarming implication is the threat to food security. Southern Tagalog is one of the most productive fruit, coconut and rice producing regions in the Philippines. If the land is to be converted to industrial use, the problem of self-sufficiency in food will be aggravated. Together with natural calamities such as typhoons, drought, and the eruption of Mt Pinatubo, a volcano in Central Luzon (considered the rice granary of Luzon), which have virtually rendered three provinces unarable for the next 10-30 years, this plan would make the food problem insurmountable. Far more urgent, we feel, is the task of resource enhancement. At Lake Laguna, for example, an aquaculture programme to enhance the threatened fishery resources would drastically reduce the price of fish in Metro Manila, and feed some 5.5 million Filipinos.

How would these grandiose development plans impinge on women? As AMIHAN's preliminary documentàtion shows, women carry the heaviest burden in such situations. With peasant families displaced from their lands—their only source of livelihood—they are left with no other recourse but to migrate to city and town centres. In most cases, males migrate but with few skills and low educational attainment, the only employment they are likely to get is contractual work in construction areas; this barely covers their families' needs for food and shelter. The women who are left behind in the provinces make do with whatever can be scraped from the land and through such marginal occupations as washing clothes, selling food and other items, and providing seasonal household help.

This kind of poverty can turn women in the countryside into commodities. There are already reports of peasant women selling their bodies in exchange for rice just to be able to feed their children. In the areas covered by the Calabarzon project, AMIHAN discovered that women have found a ready market for their sexual favours among the contractor-engineers, security men and soldiers at the project sites. It is small consolation for them that tourism projects are to be started in and around the project area. If any-thing, this will only aggravate the problem of sex commodification in the countryside.

The Green Revolution programme

In the 1960s, the Philippine agriculture sector underwent a major change when the Green Revolution, a global campaign to increase agricultural pro-duction, was introduced. Women, who traditionally practised indigenous, environmentally sound methods of planting and nurturing through the use of natural fertilisers and pesticides, were alienated from these traditional technologies through the intervention of the Green Revolution. Further-more, impoverished peasant families were forced to allocate a substantial part of their paltry farm income to pay for high-cost chemical fertilisers and pesticides.

Integral to the implementation of the Green Revolution was the introduc-tion of high-yielding varieties (HYVs) of seeds that required an abundant use of fertilisers and water in order to yield. With chemical inputs, agricul-tural harvests did pick up, but the nation's self-sufficiency in food, particu-larly rice, remained elusive. As more farmers used the HYVs, however, demand for fertilisers and pesticides grew, as a result of which the country became heavily dependent on imports which now make up 70 per cent of the country's total supply.

More disturbing than this dependency, however, are the effects of chemical fertilisers and pesticides on the fertility of the soil and the health of peasants, particularly women. Apart from their economic displacement, women are now being alienated from and threatened in a function that is exclusively theirs: reproduction. Women farm-workers in the pineapple and banana plantations in Mindanao, and rice and corn workers, were the first to notice that prolonged exposure to certain pesticides can actually cause spontaneous abortions and stillbirths. At the very least, they cause chronic dizziness and malaise, blurred vision, peeling off of nails and skin, and swelling of the legs.

Farmers have also testified, as substantiated in scientific studies, that soil fertility is adversely affected and the natural balance of organic nutrients destroyed. Traditional and affordable foods—snails, frogs and varieties of fish such as mudfish and milkfish—have been exterminated; in their place, new pests which can only be controlled by chemical pesticides have emerged and proliferated.

We will take just one example, that of the golden apple snail, which was introduced into the Philippines by a Taiwanese company. This was hailed as a product with a good export potential and, because of its high protein content, as a good substitute for those with a protein-poor diet, locally. But before long, it had reared its ugly head. The golden apple snail found its way to the rice fields and unleashed its havoc on rice stalks. According to the peasants, a hectare of golden apple snail-infested field can be destroyed in a single night.

Transnational companies rushed to the 'rescue' and offered up Brestan and Aquatin, two brands of molluscides which undoubtedly worked miracles in the farmers' rice fields. But that was not the end of the story. Apart from their potency and effectiveness in eliminating snails, the molluscides also damage human flesh. Prolonged contact with water treated with these molluscides causes human flesh and nails to itch, burn and even peel off. There is also clear evidence to show that contact with treated water in the rice fields, where women do all the transplanting, weeding and harvesting, causes a swelling of the genitals and legs. Brestan and Aquatin were banned by the Fertilizer and Pesticides Authority of the Department of Agriculture of the Philippines in mid-1990 but have been available under the counter after the banning.

Women's initiative for a better future

All is not gloom for Filipino peasant women, however. Apart from the political struggles, initiatives have been taken to re-order farm technology and production and make them more sensitive to the needs of women and the environment. These initiatives have drawn on the experiences and experiments of the women themselves. AMIHAN has begun a pilot study of organic and integrated farming systems in two demonstration farms it started in 1992. One, located in Bulacan, a province north of Manila, concentrates on rice and vegetable production while the other, which falls within the Calabarzon area, keeps livestock and has started fruit and vegetable farming. One AMIHAN member in Cebu, in fact, did away with the use of chemical farm inputs long ago, and started using organic farming methods; it took her only about two years to restore the lost fertility of her land.

Alternative methods of pest control are being evolved by women peasants. Water used for washing clothes or that treated with a coconut-based soap produced by the women themselves is now used as a pesticide for different kinds of plants. Integrated pest management is also underway. Among other things, this makes use of indigenous plants which, when planted between eggplants and other vegetable crops, keep pests away. In most cases, the vegetables which women grow in their backyards, primarily for domestic consumption, do not use chemical fertilisers or pesticides. Various measures, including the use of compost baskets, are helping to maintain the fertility of the soil in these lands.

In order to improve women's health the AMIHAN chapter in Isabela developed a stove made of stone, which draws smoke from firewood away from the person using it. Smoke inhalation is therefore minimised.

AMIHAN is committed to limiting the use of chemical fertilisers and pesticides and to rehabilitating the soil through more sustainable methods of farming. It has shared these ideas with other peasant organisations, but there is some resistance on their part, which we believe arises partly from the uncertainty of the proffered option. The peasants fear that the shift to sustainable, non-chemical agricultural practice may diminish the land's productivity and their income. They are also inhibited by the responsibilities and risks that need to be dealt with; exercising such an option would mean directly confronting giant transnational corporations whose profit interests are at stake, and the Philippines government, which is committed to guaranteeing maximum satisfaction to foreign investors.

At this point, AMIHAN's is practically a voice in the wilderness. For the moment, our greatest responsibility is in communicating peasant women's experiences and options in a language that peasant organisations, advocates and the government can understand, and perhaps relate to and sympathise with. For without this, ours may well continue to be the lone voice.

Ethnic Conflict in Sri Lanka
Its Ecological and Political Consequences

Rita Sebastian

Background to the conflict

Sri Lanka's ethnic conflict has manifested itself at various levels, and the sociological and ecological degradation has been no less devastating in its impact than the political and military fall-out. For wars, whatever their degree of intensity, destabilise institutions, affect human relations and destroy and damage the physical environment.

The 25,332-square-mile island is home to a multi-ethnic, multi-religious and multi-lingual population of 17 million people. Sinhala Buddhists comprise 75 per cent of the population, Tamils 13 per cent, Muslims seven per cent and various smaller ethnic groups the rest.

The politics of ethnic confrontation in the island between the Sinhala majority and the Tamil minority has a long and chequered history. According to the Sri Lankan historian, K.M. de Silva: 'What distinguished elite politics in Sri Lanka in the first two decades of the 20th century from the succeeding decades was the harmony that prevailed between the Sinhalese and Tamil leadership'.

In the political jargon of the day, there were two majority communities, the Sinhalese and the Tamils, and the minorities were the smaller racial groups. The situation changed fundamentally after 1922 when, instead of two majority communities, there emerged one majority community—the Sinhalese— with the Tamils regarding themselves as a minority. This has remained the case ever since.

Grievances, real and imaginary, were numerous. There were allegations of minority discrimination, under-representation of minority Tamils in the administrative services, the exclusion of students from the university through unfair marking of examination papers.

Nineteen fifty-six saw the rise of a strong Sinhalese nationalist movement, led—ironically enough—by the Oxford-educated Prime Minister, S.D.R. Bandaranaike. He promised 'Sinhala only' in 24 hours. His 'Sinhala Only' Bill caused race riots, making him realise what linguistic nationalism would lead to in a plural society. English, which had for so long been the medium of education, was replaced by Sinhala and Tamil. Soon a visible divide between the communities had been created; children were compartmentalised into Sinhala and Tamil streams, and the language barrier stood effectively in the way of communal integration. Sinhala nationalism, in turn, gave rise to Tamil nationalism.

At the 1977 general elections the moderate Tamil leadership, the Tamil United Liberation Front (TULF), sought a mandate for a separate state, but after being voted into parliament the party distanced itself from the separate homeland concept. It was then that the younger and more militant groups began to formulate their own designs for liberating what they regarded as their traditional homelands, the north and east of the island. The ballot was replaced by the bullet.

The conflict breaks out

Then came 1983. A communal holocaust, the likes of which was never seen in the country before, further alienated the Tamil community. The brutal killing of an estimated 2,000 Tamils by violent Sinhala mobs, led to further bitter division. Thousands of Tamils fled to neighbouring India; others sought political asylum in the North.

Tamil militants began their deadly game of preparing for battle. They crossed the 14-mile strip of water between India and Sri Lanka at will, ferrying men and arms and other military equipment, and from their jungle hideouts in the island's north-east provinces they waged a relentless guerrilla war against government forces.

In May 1987, however, when the Sri Lankan forces launched 'Operation Liberation' to take control of the rebel stronghold of northern Jaffna, India stepped in, called a halt to the operation and, in July, in a dramatic turn of events, brokered a peace pact with the Sri Lanka government to end the conflict.

The peace pact divided the nation further. A left-wing Sinhala militant group, the Janatha Vimukthi Peramuna (JVP, or People's Liberation Front), comprising mainly of youth from the impoverished landless peasantry of the south, rose in revolt against what they perceived to be India's grand designs in the region. An estimated 8,000 Indian troops arrived in the island's north-east to monitor the cessation of hostilities and people really believed that war had finally ended. Subsequent events belied all hopes of a truce.

For over a decade now in the north and east of the island, society has been reorganised according to the new and savage imperatives of ethnic conflict and hatred. The traditionally conservative Tamils have seen their caste-bound society become militarised, and a new caste of ruthless militants has emerged, with the Tamil Tigers—the Liberation Tigers of Tamil Elaam (LTTE)—as the dominant group. These have the makings of a new class, freed from the constraints of traditional caste and morality, fiercely insular, contemptuous of institutions like the traditional judiciary and administration and, above all, believing in the dictum that all power must emanate from the barrel of a gun.

Democratic institutions have yielded to a new style of social and political fascism in which the leader's word and the party's goals override every other rational and ethical consideration. Pluralism has been rejected. Opposition of any kind is considered reasonable and history has been rewritten in keeping with current propaganda needs and demands. Paradoxically, the political culture of Tamil political liberalism, which produced such eminent leaders as Ponnambalam Ramanathan and Ponnambalam Arunachalam, has come abruptly to an end. It has been replaced by an unyielding and uncompromising generation of young men and women, nurtured in the politics of a militant nationalism.

In the last decade, nationalism has given rise to armed conflict. The ravages of that conflict are most conspicuous in the physical desolation which has overtaken the north-east provinces. The Jaffna peninsula itself, and other towns on the periphery considered to be cradles of Tamil culture, resemble European cities after the second world war. It is as if the peninsula has been flung back into some kind of medieval degradation visible in the damaged and destroyed buildings, twisted steel and heaped rubble.

The major part of the destruction has come in what could be classified as three major waves of confrontations beginning from the early 1980s. There was the first phase of militants, several groups of them, battling the Sri Lankan forces in the north-east. Next came foreign troops in the form of an Indian Peace Keeping Force (IPKF) following the signing of the controversial Indo-Lanka Accord in July 1987. And with the breakdown of the 13-month peace dialogue between the government and the LTTE in June 1990, the war was on again.

The only overall assessment of war damage to date was carried out by a World Bank team which visited the island following the signing of the peace pact after four years of intensified fighting between Tamil militants and government forces. Non-governmental organisations (NGOs) have, however, made efforts to assess the damage in specific areas to which they have had access, and government agents have collected piecemeal data in various districts.

The World Bank team reported:

About 7,000 lives were lost and thousands more wounded. Almost 100,000 families or about 500,000 people lost their homes. The northern and eastern parts of the country suffered the greatest disruptions. Many workplaces were destroyed or damaged. Not only were urban areas affected but fighting was widespread in the rural areas as well. Thousands of farmers were forced to leave their lands, and the irrigation systems they were so dependent on were damaged. Fishermen lost their boats and whole fishing villages were destroyed. Schools, hospitals and clinics were damaged resulting in serious hardships to children and patients.

The World Bank team estimated the damage to infrastructure at USD 700 million, but made the point that this was only a portion of the quantifiable economic losses the country had suffered. All in all, according to the World Bank team, the losses to the country amounted to well over USD 2 billion and the overall rehabilitation and reconstruction effort would cost RS 13 billion (USD 388.4 million).

The programme was to be phased out over a 3-year period. Tragically for the country the programme never got off the ground. The fragile peace did not hold and in October 1987 the LTTE reneged on the peace pact, provoking an Indian offensive against them.

Controlling an area meant controlling access to it. To prevent the Indian forces doing this the Tamil militants blew up bridges, destroyed culverts and mined roads. They removed miles of railway sleepers, felled hundreds of coconut and other trees to build a sophisticated network of underground bunkers, military training camps and hospitals for their fighters. The forests were their domain and they ravaged them at will.

An estimated 70,000 Indian soldiers virtually took over the towns and villages in the north-east. Their innumerable camps, sandbagged sentry points and watchtowers converted the open sprawling countryside into well-secured fortresses. And as the battle escalated, advancing platoons of soldiers mowed down anything that impeded their progress, house, tree or animal.

The war spawned other problems. The government set up new settlement schemes, clearing acres of virgin jungle. Forests that grew along the sides of roads were scorched to prevent surprise rebel ambushes.

While the state has been actively engaged in a massive island-wide national forestry development project, its activities in the north-east have been severely hampered. There have been hardly any forestry extension activities in the Jaffna, Mullaitivu or Vavuniya districts in the north, or in Batticaloa, Trincomalee or Ampara in the east. The forests in the north-east where the women collected fuelwood are no longer accessible, having become part of the theatre of continuing military operations.

NGOs and the role of women

In Sri Lanka, environmental organisations have tended to be urban-oriented but, in the last couple of years, the damage to the environment has become the concern of rural groups. The Environment Congress is an umbrella organisation of 161 rural-based associations. Other community development non-governmental organisations and women's groups are concerned with environmental issues, but the environment by itself is not the primary or most urgent concern. Among the rural poor there are other more urgent priorities such as income generation, nutrition and children's welfare. The only all-women environmental group, the Sinhala Demala Gemi Kantha Sammelanaya (Sinhala-Tamil Women's Network), has as its main objective the promotion of understanding between the two communities rather than 'improving the environment'.

It can truly be said that this war has been cruel above all to the women. The recruitment of women into the militant movements has brought about a radical transformation of the role of woman as wife and mother. In several of the battles against government forces, the women's wing of the LTTE, the 'Freedom Birds', have been as deadly as their male counterparts. The woman suicide bomber responsible for the assassination of the Indian Prime Minister, Rajiv Gandhi, symbolises the extent of that transformation. Women on motor-bicycles, with automatic weapons slung across their shoulders, or at the wheel of heavy trucks are a common sight in the northern peninsula, virtual LTTE territory. No different from their male counterparts, they have adopted the gun as the symbol of their liberation.

Rajani Thiranagama, a female academic cruelly gunned down by the LTTE, gives a graphic description of the women cadres in the book she co-authored with other academics of Jaffna University, entitled *The Broken Palmyrah: The Tamil Crisis in Sri Lanka*.

One cannot but be inspired when one sees the women of the LTTE, two by two in the night, with their AK's slung over their shoulders, patrolling the entrances to Jaffna ... one could see the nationalist fervour and the romantic vision of women in arms defending the nation. This becomes a great draw for other women....

Our social set-up, its restrictions on creative expression for women and the evils of the dowry system are some of the social factors that led to their initial recruitment. Moreover, the political climate created by the struggle in the past decade and the increasing loss of men to state terrorism and to the world at large as refugees and emigrants are some of the contributing factors necessitating women's recruitment.

The militant groups had no problems with recruitment in the initial stages although, later, forced conscription drove young men out of the country. Stories of teenagers, both girls and boys, leaving home with only a note indicating to their bewildered parents that they had joined the militants, are legion. *The Broken Palmyrah* tells us:

One often finds amongst intelligent middle class girls a reckless emotional drive to serve a cause like the LTTE's. Being very articulate speakers, they bring in village girls who wish to imitate them. But the middle class girls soon get frustrated by fascist tendencies in the organisation and opt out.

The Broken Palmyrah also records a difference in behaviour, and attitude to militancy, between rural and urban women.

The natural defiance of the women from the lower classes remained a remarkable feature as opposed to the pliability of upper class women. Village women in the east went out with rice pounders to stop the internecine fighting during the LTTE and EPRLF* clash. When the LTTE took on the EPRLF on December 4, 1986, women from some low class villages in Jaffna defied the LTTE by sitting on the roads armed with kitchen knives and chilli powder. The same women were to prove a nightmare to the Indians when they arrived.

The arrival of the Indian forces inflicted another trauma on the already victimised women. There were several allegations of rape and molestation, most of them occurring during house-to-house searches for the LTTE. To the Indian Peace Keeping Force (IPKF) every Tamil male was identified as a member of LTTE. It was an obsession which coloured their judgment in dealing with a civilian population trapped between the warring sides.

There were two distinct developments that arose out of Tamil militancy in the north, which in its totality may be considered positive. Militancy broke through the rigid caste barriers, specially in the northern Jaffna peninsula where the lower castes suffered greatly through repressive practices. It also gave rise to an assertive women's movement. When large numbers of youth began disappearing the women banded themselves into a 'Mothers' Front'. The women came from all kinds of society, organising rallies and picketing public officials, to make for an active protest campaign. But it soon lost momentum, and as the authors of *The Broken Palmyrah* tell us:

In later years with the increasing hegemony of the LTTE and the suppression of all democratic organisations through pressure to toe the line, the Front, pushed into political conformism, lost its wide appeal and militancy. It became another Y.W.C.A. (Young Women's Christian Association).... Sadly, the Jaffna Mothers' Front's inarticulate acceptance of women's sufferings at the hands of the IPKF and, earlier, the LTTE's inwardly directed violence leaves them in a wasteland only to be used as a tool by one force and disregarded and bullied by the other.

However, there emerged several other women's organisations which took on the rehabilitation of literally hundreds of women who lost their husbands to the war. It is a challenging role for the women who have had to shoulder the responsibility of young families, of learning new skills, of re-fashioning their lives.

Rajeswarie is a young widow of 27 with a four-year old child. Two years ago her husband disappeared without a trace in eastern Batticaloa. She fled the war-ravaged town to seek shelter in Colombo. Today she lives in a refugee camp maintained by the state where 700 women share a single toilet. Two of

---

* Eelam People's Revolutionary Liberation Front—ex-militants who have since entered mainstream politics.

her sisters, young widows themselves, are also refugees. Rajeswarie was married to a Tamil, her sisters to Sinhalese. She believes the state forces took her husband. Her two brothers-in-law were killed by the LTTE.

Another woman, another story, which have been recorded by 'University Teachers for Human Rights', a human rights group of academics.

On August 26, 1991, Chelvi was arrested by the LTTE. Chelvi was involved in women's issues and acted in plays. She was once involved in the women's section of the People's Liberation Organisation of Tamil Eelam (PLOTE) and when that organisation degenerated to the level of torturing a large number of its cadres, she became disillusioned and left the organisation. She came back and joined the university to do her degree. She was very much involved in various social activities including being a member of the university women's organisation and very much concerned about the direction of the struggle. The LTTE has not given any reason for her arrest.

Women still face arbitrary arrest and are still the main victims of the war. Half the 600,000 internally displaced persons, most of them in state-run welfare centres, are women and children.

Sadly the quality-of-life index for which Sri Lanka was once famed and which put Sri Lanka ahead of all South Asia has been destroyed beyond present repair.

The strongly cohesive Tamil community is now scattered in many lands. Ironically, the Tamils do not seem to have an insight into the searing nature of their predicament, and blame bogey figures like India and the Sinhala majority. Some follow rigidly Marxist ideologies while others find comfort in Tamil nationalism. It is a bewildered community bereft of enlightened leadership and most aptly symbolised by Tamil refugees being tossed around like human shuttlecocks not only in Europe but also in neighbouring India.

The Seed and the Earth
Biotechnology and the Colonisation of Regeneration

Vandana Shiva

Regeneration lies at the heart of life, and has been the central principle guiding sustainable societies; without renewal there can be no sustainability. However, modern industrial society has no time for thinking about regeneration, and therefore no space for living regeneratively. Its devaluation of the processes of regeneration are the cause of both the ecological crisis and the crisis of non-sustainability.

The continuity between regeneration in human and non-human nature that was the basis of all ancient world-views was broken by patriarchy. Man was separated from nature, and the creativity involved in processes of regeneration was denied. Creativity became the monopoly of men, who were considered to be engaged in 'production', while women were engaged in mere 'reproduction' or 'procreation' which, rather than being treated as *renewable* production, was looked upon as non-production.

Activity, as purely male, was constructed on the separation of the earth from the seed and on the association of an 'inert' and empty earth with the passivity of the female. The symbols of the seed and the earth therefore undergo a metamorphosis when cast in a patriarchal mould; with it are restructured gender relations and our perception of nature and its regeneration. This non-ecological view of nature and culture has formed the basis of patriarchal perceptions of gender roles in reproduction across religions and through the ages.

The passivity of the earth and the activity of the seed are patriarchal constructs. This gendered seed/earth metaphor is then applied to human production and reproduction to make the relationship of dominance of men over women appear 'natural'. But the 'naturalness' of this hierarchy is built on a material/spiritual dualism, with maleness artificially associated with pure spirit and femaleness constructed as merely material, bereft of spirit. As Bachofen has stated,

> The triumph of paternity brings with it the liberation of the spirit from the manifestations of nature, a sublimation of human existence over the laws of material life. Maternity pertains to the physical side of man, the only thing he shares with animals; the paternal spiritual principle belongs to him alone. Triumphant paternity partakes of the heavenly light, while child-bearing motherhood is bound up with the earth that bears all things.[1]

Central to the assumption of men's superiority over women in patriarchy is the social construct of passivity/materiality as female and animal, and activity/spirituality as male and distinctly human: this is reflected in dualisms like mind/body, with the mind being non-material, male and active, and the body physical, female and passive. It is also reflected in the dualism of culture/nature, and the assumption that men alone have access to culture as women are 'bound up with the earth that bears all things'.[2] What these artificial dichotomies obscure is that activity, not passivity, is nature's nature.

By focusing on seeds and women's bodies as sites of regeneration this contribution attempts to look at how the new biotechnologies are reproducing these old patriarchal divisions of activity/passivity, culture/nature. It will also examine how these dichotomies are then used as instruments of capitalist patriarchy to colonise the regeneration of plants and human beings. Finally, it is an effort towards reclaiming the activity and creativity of women and nature in a non-patriarchal mould by *decolonising* regeneration.

New colonies, new creation boundaries

The land, the forests, the rivers, the oceans, the atmosphere have all been colonised, eroded and polluted. Capital now has to look for new colonies to invade and exploit for its further accumulation. These new colonies are, in my view, the interior spaces of the bodies of women, plants and animals.

The invasion and take-over of land as colonies was made possible through the technology of the gunboat; the invasion and takeover of the life of organisms as the new colonies is being made possible through the technology of genetic engineering.

Biotechnology, as the handmaiden of capital in the post-industrial era, makes it possible to colonise and control that which is autonomous, free and self-regenerative. Through reductionist science, capital goes where it has never been before. The fragmentation of reductionism opens up areas for exploitation and invasion. Technological development under capitalist patriarchy proceeds steadily from what it has already transformed and used up, driven by its predatory appetite, towards that which has still not been consumed. It is in this sense that the seed and women's bodies as sites of regenerative power are, in the eyes of capitalist patriarchy, among the last colonies.[3]

While ancient patriarchy used the symbol of the active seed and the passive earth, capitalist patriarchy, through the new biotechnologies, reconstitutes the seed as passive and locates activity and creativity in the engineering mind. The reconstitution of the seed from being a regenerative source of life into valueless raw material goes hand in hand with the devaluation of those who regenerate life *of* the seed, *through* the seed—that is the farmers and peasants of the Third World—just as the reconstitution of the earth from being a living system into mere matter went hand in hand with the devaluation of the contributions of non-European cultures and nature, when land began to be colonised 500 years ago.

From *terra mater* to *terra nullius*

All sustainable cultures, in their diversity, have viewed the earth as *terra mater*. The patriarchal construct of the passivity of the earth and the consequent creation of the colonial category of land as *terra nullius*, served two purposes: it denied the existence and prior rights of original inhabitants and negated the regenerative capacity and life processes of the earth.[4] The decimation of indigenous peoples everywhere was justified morally on the grounds that they were not really human; they were part of the fauna. As Pilger has observed, the *Encyclopaedia Britannica* appeared to be in no doubt about this in the context of Australia: 'Man in Australia is an animal of prey. More ferocious than the lynx, the leopard, or the hyena, he devours his own people.'[5] In another Australian textbook, *Triumph in the Tropics*, Australian aborigines were equated with their half-wild dogs.[6] Being animals, the original Australians and Americans, the Africans and Asians possessed no rights as human beings. Their lands could be usurped as *terra nullius*—lands empty of people, 'vacant', 'waste' and 'unused'. The morality of the missions justified the military take-over of resources all over the world to serve imperial markets. European men were thus able to describe their invasions as 'discoveries', piracy and theft as 'trade', and extermination and enslavement as their 'civilising mission'.

Scientific missions colluded with religious missions to deny rights to nature. The rise of mechanical philosophy with the emergence of the scientific revolution was based on the destruction of concepts of a self-regenerative, self-organising nature which sustained all life. For Bacon, who is called the father of modern science, nature was no longer 'Mother' Nature, but a female nature, conquered by an aggressive masculine mind. As Carolyn Merchant points out, this transformation of nature from a living, nurturing mother to inert, dead and manipulable matter was eminently suited to the exploitation imperative of growing capitalism. The nurturing earth image acted as a cultural constraint on exploitation of nature. 'One does not readily slay a mother, dig her entrails or mutilate her body'. But the images of mastery and domination created by the Baconian programme and the scientific revolution removed all restraint and functioned as cultural sanctions for the denudation of nature.

The removal of animistic, organic, assumptions about the cosmos constituted the death of nature—the most far-reaching effect of the scientific revolution. Because nature was now viewed as a system of dead, inert particles moved by external, rather than inherent forces, the mechanical framework itself could legitimate the manipulation of nature. Moreover, as a conceptual framework, the mechanical order had associated with it a framework of values based on power, fully compatible with the directions taken by commercial capitalism.[7]

The construct of the inert earth began to be given a new and sinister significance as development denied the earth's productive capacity and created systems of agriculture which could not regenerate or sustain themselves.

Sustainable agriculture is based on the recycling of soil nutrients. This involves returning to the soil part of the nutrients that come from it and support plant growth. The maintenance of the nutrient cycle, and through it the fertility of the soil, is based on this inviolable law of return which recognises the earth as the source of fertility. The Green Revolution paradigm of agriculture substituted the regenerative nutrient cycle with linear flows of purchased inputs of chemical fertilisers from factories and marketed outputs of agricultural commodities. Fertility was no longer the property of soil but of chemicals. The Green Revolution was essentially based on 'miracle seeds' which needed chemical fertilisers and which did not produce plant outputs for returning to the soil.[8] The earth was again viewed as an empty vessel for holding intensive inputs of irrigated water and chemical fertilisers. The 'activity' lay in the 'miracle' seeds which transcended nature's fertility cycles.

Ecologically, however, the earth and soil were not empty, and the growth of Green Revolution varieties did not take place only with the seed-fertiliser packet. The creation of soil diseases and micro-nutrient deficiencies are an indication of the invisible demands the new varieties were making on the fertility of the soil; and desertification indicates the broken cycles of soil fertility caused by an agriculture that produces only for the market. The increase in production of grain for marketing was achieved in the Green Revolution strategy by reducing the biomass for internal use on the farm. The reduction of output for straw production was probably not considered a serious cost since chemical fertilisers were thought to be a total substitute for organic manure. Yet, as experience has shown, the fertility of soils cannot be reduced to NPK (nitrogen, phosphorus, potassium) in factories, and agricultural *productivity* necessarily *includes returning to the soil part of the biological products that the soil yields*. The seed and the earth mutually create conditions for each other's regeneration and renewal. Technologies cannot provide a *substitute* for nature and work outside nature's ecological processes without destroying the very basis of production, nor can markets provide the only measure of 'output' and 'yield'.

Biological products, which were not sold on the market but used as inputs for maintaining soil fertility, were totally ignored by the cost-benefit equations of the Green Revolution miracle. They did not appear in the list of inputs because they were not purchased, nor in the list of outputs because they were not sold. Yet what was seen as 'unproductive' or 'waste' in the commercial context of the Green Revolution is now emerging as productive in the ecological context and as the only route to sustainable agriculture. By treating essential organic inputs as 'waste', the Green Revolution strategy unwittingly ensured that fertile and productive soils were actually laid waste; the 'land-augmenting' technology has proved to be a land-degrading and land-destroying one. With the greenhouse effect and global warming, a new dimension has been added to the ecologically destructive effect of chemical fertilisers; nitrogen-based fertilisers release nitrous oxide, one of the greenhouse gases causing global warming, into the atmosphere. Chemical fertilisers have thus contributed to the erosion of food security through the pollution of land, water and the atmosphere.

From seeds of the earth to seeds of the lab

While the Green Revolution was based on the assumption that the earth is inert, the biotechnology revolution robs the seed of its fertility and self-regenerative capacities and colonises it in two major ways: firstly through technical means, and secondly through property rights. Processes like hybridisation are the technological means which stop seed from reproducing itself. This provides capital with an eminently effective way of circumventing natural constraints on the commodification of the seed. Hybrid varieties do not produce true-to-type seed, and farmers must return to the breeder each year for new seed stock.

To use Jack Kloppenburg's description of the seed: it is both a 'means of production' as well as a 'product'.[9] Whether they are tribals engaged in 'shifting cultivation' or peasants practising settled agriculture, in planting each year's crop farmers also reproduce the necessary element of their means of production. The seed thus presents capital with a simple biological obstacle; given the appropriate conditions, it reproduces itself and multiplies. Modern plant-breeding has primarily been an attempt to remove this biological obstacle, and the new biotechnologies are the latest tools for transforming what is simultaneously a 'means of production' and a 'product' into mere 'raw material'.

The hybridisation of seed was an invasion into the seed itself. As Kloppenburg has stated, it broke the unity of seed as foodgrain and as a means of production. In doing so, it opened up the space for capital accumulation that private industry needed in order to control plant breeding and commercial seed production. And, it became the source of ecological disruption by transforming a self-regenerative process into a broken linear flow of supply of living seed as raw material and a reverse flow of seed commodities as products. The decoupling of seed from grain also changes the status of seed.

The commodified seed is ecologically incomplete and ruptured at two levels: (i) it does not *reproduce* itself, while by definition, seed is a regenerative resource. Genetic resources are thus, through technology, transformed from a renewable into a non-renewable resource; (ii) it does not *produce* by itself. It needs the help of other purchased inputs to produce. As the seed and chemical companies merge, the dependence on inputs will increase. Ecologically, whether a chemical is added externally or internally, it remains an external input in the ecological cycle of the reproduction of seed. It is this shift from ecological processes of production through regeneration to technological processes of non-regenerative production that underlies the dispossession of farmers and the drastic reduction of biological diversity in agriculture. It is at the root of the creation of poverty and of non-sustainability in agriculture.

Where technological means fail to prevent farmers from reproducing their own seed, legal regulation in the form of intellectual property rights and patents is brought in. Patents are central to the colonisation of plant regeneration and, like land titles, are based on the assumption of ownership and property. A vice president of Genentech has stated, 'When you have a chance to write a clean slate, you can make some very basic claims, because the standard you are compared to is the state of prior art, and in biotechnology there just is not much.'[10] Ownership and property claims are made on living resources, but prior custody and use of those resources by farmers is not the measure against which the patent is set. Rather, it is the intervention of technology that determines the claim to their exclusive use, and the possession of this technology then becomes the reason for ownership by corporations and for the simultaneous dispossession and disenfranchisement of farmers. As *terra nullius* was divested of all prior rights, so are living resources now being divested.

As with the transformation of *terra mater* to *terra nullius*, the new biotechnologies rob farmers' seeds of life and value by the very process that makes corporate seeds the basis of wealth creation. Indigenous varieties, called landraces, evolved through both natural and human selection, and produced and used by Third World farmers worldwide, are 'primitive cultivars'; those varieties created by modern plant breeders in international research centres or by transnational seed corporations are called 'advanced' or 'elite'. Trevor Williams, the former Executive Secretary of IBPGR (International Board for Plant Genetic Resources) has argued that 'it is not the original material which produces cash returns' and a 1983 forum on plant breeding stated that 'raw germplasm only becomes valuable after considerable investment of time and money'.[11] According to this calculation, peasants' time is considered valueless and available for free. Once again a creation boundary is being arbitrarily determined to deny value to all prior processes of creation by defining them into nature. Thus, plant breeding by farmers is not breeding; it is only when farmers' varieties of 'primitive' germplasm are mixed or crossed with inbred lines in international labs by international scientists that 'creation' and 'innovation' are seen to happen:

At this point real plant breeding *begins*. That is, the long, laborious, expensive and always risky process of back crossing and other means required to first make genetic sense out of the chaos created by the foreign germplasm, and eventually make dollars and cents from a marketable product.[12]

But the landraces which farmers have developed are not genetically chaotic. They consist of improved and selected material, embodying the experience, inventiveness and hard work of farmers, past and present; and the evolutionary material processes they have undergone serve ecological and social needs. It is these needs that are undermined by the monopolising tendency of corporations. Placing the contribution of corporate scientists over and above the intellectual contribution made by Third World farmers over ten thousand years, in the areas of conservation, breeding, domestication and development of plant and animal genetic resources, is based on rank social discrimination.

Farmers' rights, plant breeders' rights and intellectual property rights

As Pat Mooney has argued, 'The perception that intellectual property is only recognisable when produced in laboratories by men in lab coats is fundamentally a racist view of scientific development',[13] for the total genetic change achieved by farmers over millennia has been far greater than that achieved during the last hundred or two hundred years of more systematic science-based efforts. The limits of the market system in assigning value can hardly be a reason for denying value to farmers' seeds and nature's seeds. It indicates the deficiencies in the logic of the market rather than the status of the seed or of farmers' intelligence.

The denial of prior rights and creativity is essential for owning life. A brief book prepared by the biotechnology industry states:

Patent laws would in effect have drawn an imaginary line around your processes and products. If any one steps over that line to use, make or sell your inventions or even if someone steps over that line in using, making or selling his own products, you could sue for patent protection.[14]

Jack Doyle has appropriately remarked that patents are less concerned with innovation than with territory, and can act as instruments of territorial takeover by claiming exclusive access to creativity and innovation and thereby monopoly rights to ownership.[15] The farmers who are the guardians of the germplasm have to be dispossessed to allow the new colonisation to happen.

As in the colonisation of land, the colonisation of life processes will have a serious impact on Third World agriculture. First, it will undermine the cultural and ethical fabric of our agriculturally based societies, in which fundamental life processes are not to be tampered with. With the introduction of patents, seeds—which have hitherto been treated as gifts and exchanged freely between farmers—will become patented commodities. Hans Leenders, former Secretary General of the International Association of Plant Breeders for the Protection of Plant Varieties (ASSINSEL), has proposed the abolition of the farmer's right to save seed. He says,

Even though it has been a tradition in most countries that a farmer can save seed from his own crop, it is under the changing circumstances not equitable that farmers can use this seed and grow a commercial crop out of it without payment of a royalty ...; the seed industry will have to fight hard for a better kind of protection.[16]

Although genetic engineering and biotechnology only relocate existing genes rather than create new ones, the ability to relocate and separate is translated into the power and right to own; the power to own a part is then translated into control of the entire organism.

The corporate demand for the conversion of a common heritage into a commodity, and for profits generated through this transformation to be treated as property rights, has serious political and economic implications for Third World farmers. They will now be forced into a three-level relationship with the corporations demanding a monopoly on life forms and life processes through patents. First, farmers are *suppliers* of germplasm to transnational corporations; second, they become *competitors* in terms of innovation and rights to genetic resources; and third, they are *consumers* of the technological and industrial products of these corporations. Patent protection displaces the farmer as a competitor, transforms him into a supplier of free raw material, and makes him totally dependent on industrial supplies for vital inputs such as seed. Above all, the frantic cry for patent protection in agriculture is for protection *from* farmers, who are the original breeders and developers of biological resources in agriculture. It is argued that patent protection is essential for innovation, but what emerges is that it is essential only for that innovation that garners profit for corporate business; after all, farmers have been making innovations for centuries, as have public institutions for decades, without property rights or patent protection.

Further, unlike plant breeders' rights (PBRs) the new utility patents are very broad-based, allowing monopoly rights over individual genes and even over characteristics. PBRs do not entail ownership of the germplasm in the seeds, they only grant a monopoly right over the selling and marketing of a specific variety. Patents, on the other hand, allow for multiple claims that may cover not only whole plants, but plant parts and processes as well. So, according to attorney Anthony Diepenbrock, 'You could file for protection of a few varieties of crops, their macro-parts (flowers, fruits, seeds and so on), their micro-parts (cells, genes, plasmids and the like) and whatever novel processes you develop to work 'these parts, all using one multiple claim'. [17]

Patent protection implies the exclusion of farmers' rights over resources having these genes and characteristics. This will undermine the very foundations of agriculture. For example, a patent has been granted in the US to a biotechnology company, Sungene, for a sunflower variety with very high oleic acid content. The claim allowed was for the characteristic (i.e. high oleic acid) and not just for the genes producing the characteristic. Sungene has notified others involved in sunflower breeding that the development of any variety high in oleic acid will be considered an infringement of its patent.

The landmark event for the patenting of plants was the 1985 judgment in the US, now famous as *ex parte Hibberd*, in which 'molecular genetics' scientist Kenneth Hibberd and his co-inventors 'were granted patents on the tissue culture, seed, and whole plant of a corn line selected from tissue culture'. [18] The Hibberd application included over 260 separate claims, which give the molecular genetics scientists the right to exclude others from use of all 260 aspects. While Hibberd apparently provides a new legal context for corporate competition, the most profound impact will be felt in the competition between farmers and the seed industry.

As Kloppenburg has indicated, with Hibberd, a juridical framework is now in place that may allow the seed industry to realise one of its longest held and most cherished goals, that of forcing all farmers of any crop to buy seed every year instead of obtaining it through reproduction. Industrial patents allow the right to *use* the product, not to *make* it. Since seed makes itself, a strong utility patent for seed implies that a farmer purchasing patented seed would have the right to use (to grow) the seed, but not to make seed (to save and replant). If the Dunkel Draft of the General Agreement on Tariffs and Trade (GATT) is implemented, the farmer who saves and replants the seed of a patented or protected plant variety will be violating the law.

Through intellectual property rights an attempt is made to take away what belongs to nature, to farmers, to women, and to term this invasion 'improvement' and 'progress'. Violence and plunder as instruments of wealth creation do not just belong to the history of colonisation, which began 500 years ago with the early invasions; they are essential to the colonisation of nature and of our bodies through the new technologies. As before, those who are exploited become the criminals, those who exploit require protection. The North must be protected from the South so that it can continue its uninterrupted theft of the Third World's genetic diversity. The 'seed wars', trade wars, patent 'protection' and intellectual property rights at GATT are modern versions of claims to ownership through separation and fragmentation. The US International Trade Commission estimates that US industry is losing anything between USD 100 and 300 billion due to the absence of intellectual property rights. If this regime of 'rights' being demanded by the US comes into being, the transfer of funds from poor to rich countries will exacerbate the Third World crisis ten times over.[19]

The US has accused the Third World of 'piracy'. The estimates provided for royalties lost in agricultural chemicals are USD 202 million and USD 2,545 million for pharmaceuticals.[20] However, as the team at RAFI, the Rural Advancement Foundation International, in Canada has shown, if the contribution of Third World peasants and tribals is taken into account, the roles are dramatically reversed: the US owes USD 302 million in royalties for agriculture and 5,097 million for pharmaceuticals to Third World countries, according to these latter estimates. In other words, in these two biological industry sectors alone, the US owes 2.7 billion dollars to the Third World.[21] It is to prevent these debts from being taken into account that it becomes essential to set up the creation boundary through the regulation of intellectual property rights; without it, the colonisation of the regenerative processes of life renewal is impossible. Yet if this too is allowed to happen in the name of patent protection, innovation and progress, life itself will have been colonised.

There are, at present, two trends reflecting different views as to how native seeds, indigenous knowledge and farmers' rights should be treated. On the one hand are initiatives across the world that recognise the inherent value of seeds and biodiversity, acknowledge the contribution of farmers to agricultural innovation and seed conservation, and see patents as a threat both to genetic diversity and to farmers. At the global level the most significant platforms to have made the issue of farmers' rights visible are the FAO Commission on Plant Genetic Resources[22] and the Keystone Dialogue.[23] At the local level, communities all over Asia, Africa and Latin America are taking steps to save and regenerate their native seeds. Only to mention one example, we have in India set up a network called 'Navdanya' for the conservation of people's seeds.

Despite these initiatives, however, the dominant trend continues to be towards the displacement of local plant diversity and its substitution by patented varieties; at the same time, international agencies under pressure from seed corporations are pushing for regimes of intellectual property rights which deny farmers their intellect and their rights. The March 1991 revision of the International Convention for the Protection of New Varieties of Plants, for example, allows countries to remove the 'farmers' exemption'—the right to save and replant seed—at their discretion.[24]

In another development leading to the privatisation of genetic resources, the Consultative Group on International Agricultural Research (CGIAR) made a policy statement on 22 May, 1992 allowing the privatisation and patenting of genetic resources held in international gene banks.[25] The strongest pressure for patents is coming from GATT, especially in relation to the agreement on Trade Related Intellectual Property Rights (TRIPs) and Agriculture.[26]

Engineering humans

Just as technology changes seed from a living, renewable resource into mere raw material, it devalues women in a similar way. The medicalisation of reproduction has been linked to the mechanisation of the female body in which a set of fragmented, fetishised and replaceable parts are managed by professional experts. While this medicalisation is most advanced in the US, it is also spreading to the Third World.

The mechanisation of childbirth is evident in the increased use of Caesarean sections. Significantly, this method, which requires the most 'management' by the doctor and the least 'labour' by the woman, is seen as providing the best product. But Caesarean sections are a surgical procedure, and the chances of complications are two to four times greater than during normal vaginal delivery. They were introduced as a means of delivering bodies at risk but when they are done routinely, they can pose an unnecessary threat to health and even life. Close to one in every four Americans is now born by Caesarean section.[27] Brazil has one of the highest proportions of Caesarean section deliveries in the world; a nationwide study of patients enrolled in the social security system showed an increase in the proportion of Caesarean sections from 15 per cent in 1974 to 31 per cent in 1980. In urban areas, such as the city of Sao Paulo, rates as high as 75 per cent have been observed. However, in several European countries there is a counter trend, a return to home births and natural childbirth.

As with plant regeneration, where agriculture has moved from the Green Revolution technologies to biotechnology, so too with human reproduction, a parallel shift is taking place. With the introduction of new reproductive technologies, the relocation of knowledge and skills from the mother to the doctor, from women to men will be accentuated. Singer and Wells, in *Having Babies*, have suggested that the production of sperm is worth a great deal more than the production of eggs. They conclude that sperm vending places a greater strain on the man than egg 'donation' does on the woman, in spite of the chemical and mechanical invasion of her body.[28]

While, currently, in vitro fertilisation (IVF) and other technologies are offered for 'abnormal' cases of infertility, the boundary between nature and non-nature is fluid and normality has a tendency to be redefined as abnormality, as technologies created for abnormal cases become more widely used. When pregnancy was first transformed into a medical disease, professional management was limited to abnormal cases, while normal cases continued to be looked after by the original professional, the midwife. While 70 per cent of childbirths were thought normal enough to be delivered at home in the UK in the 1930s, by the 1950s the same percentage were identified as abnormal enough to be delivered in hospital!

The old metaphor of women as the passive field is renewed with the new reproductive technologies. Medical developments have simply provided contemporary scientific rhetoric for the reassertion of an enduring set of deeply patriarchal beliefs. The idea of women as vessels, and the foetus as 'created' by the father's seed and owned by patriarchal right, leads logically to the breaking of organic links between the mother and the foetus.

Medical specialists, falsely believing that they 'produce' and 'create' babies, force their knowledge on knowing mothers. They treat their own knowledge as infallible, and women's knowledge as wild hysteria. And through their fragmented and invasive knowledge they create 'maternal foetal conflict' in which life is seen only in the foetus, and the mother is reduced to a potential criminal threatening her baby's life.

The medical construction of 'life' through technology is often inconsistent with the living experience of women as thinking and knowing human beings. When such conflicts arise, patriarchal science and law have worked hand in hand to establish the control by professional men over women's lives, as demonstrated by recent work on surrogacy and the new reproductive technologies. Women's rights, linked with their regenerative capacities, have been replaced by those of doctors as 'producers' and rich infertile couples as 'consumers'.

The woman whose body is being exploited as a machine is not seen as the one who needs protection from exploiting doctors and rich couples. Instead, the 'consumer', the adoptive male parent needs protection from the biological mother who has been reduced to a surrogate uterus, as in the famous Baby M. case, in which Mary Beth agreed to loan her uterus, but after experiencing what having a baby meant, wanted to return the money and keep the baby. However, a New Jersey judge ruled that a man's contract with a woman concerning his sperm is sacred and that pregnancy and childbirth are not. Commenting on this notion of 'justice', Phyllis Chesler, in her book *Sacred Bond*, says, 'It's as if these experts were 19th century missionaries and Mary Beth a particularly stubborn native who refused to convert to civilisation, and what's more, refused to let them plunder her natural resources without a fight.'[29]

The role of man as creator has also been taken to absurd lengths in an application submitted for a patent for the characterisation of the gene sequence coding for human relaxin, a hormone which is synthesised and stored in female ovaries and helps in dilation, thus facilitating the birth process. A naturally occurring substance in women's bodies is thus being treated as an 'invention' of three male scientists, Peter John Hud, Hugh David Nill, and Geoffrey William Tregear.[30] 'Ownership' is thus acquired through invasive and fragmenting technology, and it is this link between fragmenting technology and control and ownership of resources and people that forms the basis of the patriarchal project of knowledge as power over others.

Such a project is based on the acceptance of three separations: (i) the separation of mind and body; (ii) the gendered separation of male activity as intellectual and female activity as biological; and (iii) the separation of the knower and the known. These separations allow the political construction of a creation boundary that divides the thinking, active male from the unthinking, passive female, and from nature.

Biotechnology is today's dominant cultural instrument for carving out the boundary between nature and culture through intellectual property rights and for defining women's and farmers' knowledge and work into nature. These patriarchal constructs are projected as natural although there is nothing natural about them. As Claudia von Werlhof has pointed out, from the dominant standpoint, 'nature' is everything that should be available free or as cheaply as possible. This includes the products of social labour. The labour of women and Third World farmers is said to be non-labour, mere biology, a natural resource; their products are thus akin to natural deposits.[31]

The production boundary and the creation boundary

The transformation of value into disvalue, labour into non-labour, knowledge, into non-knowledge, is achieved by two very powerful constructs, the production boundary and the creation boundary. The production boundary is a political construct which excludes regenerative, renewable production cycles from the domain of production. National accounting systems which are used for calculating growth through gross national product are based on the assumption that if producers consume what they produce, they do not in fact produce at all, because they fall outside the production boundary.[32] All women who produce for their families, children and nature are thus all treated as non-productive, as economically inactive. Discussions at the UN Conference on Environment and Development (UNCED) on issues of biodiversity have also referred to production for own consumption as a 'market failure' (Agenda 21).[33] Self-sufficiency in the economic domain is therefore seen as economic deficiency when economies are confined to the market place. The devaluation of women's work, and of work done in subsistence economies in the Third World, is the natural outcome of a production boundary constructed by capitalist patriarchy.

The creation boundary does to knowledge what the production boundary does to work: it excludes the creative contributions of women and Third World peasants and tribals and treats them as being engaged in unthinking, repetitive, biological processes. The separation of production from reproduction, the characterisation of the former as economic and the latter as biological, are some of the underlying assumptions that are treated as 'natural' even though they have been socially and politically constructed.

This patriarchal shift in the creation boundary is misplaced for many reasons. First, the assumption that male activity is true creation because it takes place *ex nihilo* is ecologically false. No technological artefact or industrial commodity is formed out of nothing; no industrial process takes place where nothing was before. Nature and its creativity and other people's social labour are consumed at every level of industrial production as 'raw material' or 'energy'. The biotech seed which is treated as 'creation' to be protected by patents could not exist without the farmer's seed. The assumption that only industrial production is truly creative because it produces from nothing hides the ecological destruction that goes with it. The patriarchal creation boundary allows ecological destruction to be perceived as creation, and ecological regeneration and creation to be perceived as non-creation. This devaluing of regeneration underlies the breakdown of ecological cycles and the crisis of sustainability. To sustain life means, above all, to regenerate life; but according to the patriarchal view, to regenerate is *not* to create, it is merely to 'repeat'.

Such a definition of creativity is also false because it fails to see that women's and subsistence producers' work go into child rearing and cultivation, and because their knowledge and work are based on participation they make for the conservation of regenerative capacity.

The assumption of creation as the production of novelty is also false because no regeneration is mere repetition. It involves diversity, while engineering produces uniformity. Regeneration is how diversity is produced and renewed, in fact. While no industrial process takes place out of nothing, the creation myth of patriarchy is particularly unfounded in the case of biotechnologies where life forms are the 'raw material' for industrial production.

Rebuilding connections

The source of patriarchal power over women and nature lies in separation and fragmentation. Nature is separated from and subjugated to culture; mind is separated from and elevated above matter; female is separated from male, and identified with nature and matter. The domination over women and nature is one outcome, the disruption of cycles of regeneration is another; disease and ecological destruction arise from this interruption of the cycles of renewal of life and health. The crisis of health and ecology suggests that the assumption of man's ability to totally engineer the world, including seeds and women's bodies, is in question. Nature is not the essentialised passive construct that patriarchy assumes it to be. Ecology forces us to recognise the disharmonies and harmonies in our interactions with nature. Understanding and sensing connections and relationships is the ecological imperative.

The main contribution of the ecology movement has been the awareness that there is no separation between mind and body, human and nature. Nature is constituted in the relationships and connections that provide the very conditions for our life and health. This politics of connection and regeneration provides an alternative to the politics of separation and fragmentation that are causing ecological breakdown, and is one of solidarity with nature. This implies a radical transformation of nature and culture such that they are mutually permeating, not separate and oppositional. By stating a partnership with nature in the politics of regeneration, women are simultaneously reclaiming their own and nature's activity and creativity. There is nothing essentialist about this politics because it is, in fact, based on denying the patriarchal definition of passivity as the essence of women and nature. There is nothing absolutist about it because the 'natural' is constructed through diverse relationships in diverse settings. Natural agriculture and natural childbirth involve human creativity and sensitivity of the highest order, a creativity and knowledge emerging from partnership and participation, not separation. The politics of partnership with nature, as it is being shaped in the everyday lives of women and communities, is a politics of rebuilding connections and of regeneration through dynamism and diversity.

Notes

1. Weigle, Marta, *Creation and Procreation*, University of Philadelphia, Pennsylvania Press, 1989.
2. Weigle, Marta, *op. cit.*
3. Von Werlhof, Claudia, 'Women and nature in capitalism' in Mies, Maria (ed.), *Women: The Last Colony*, Zed Books, London, 1988.
4. Pilger, John, *A Secret Country*, Vintage, London, 1989.
5. Pilger, John, *op. cit.*
6. Pilger, John, *op. cit.*
7. Merchant, Carolyn, *The Death of Nature: Women, Ecology and the Scientific Revolution*, Harper & Row, New York, 1980.
8. Shiva, Vandana, *The Violence of the Green Revolution*, Third World Network, Penang, 1991.
9. Kloppenburg, Jack, *First the Seed*, Cambridge University Press, Cambridge, 1988.
10. Quoted in Doyle, Jack, *Altered Harvest*, Viking, New York, 1985, p. 310.
11. Quoted in Kloppenburg, *op. cit.*, p. 185.

12. Witt, Stephen, *Biotechnology and Genetic Diversity*, California Agricultural Lands Project, San Fransisco, California, 1985.
13. Mooney, Pat, 'From Cabbages to Kings' in *Development Dialogue* 1988:1-2 and Proceedings of Conference on Patenting of Life Forms, ICDA, Brussels, 1989.
14. Witt, Stephen, *op. cit.*
15. Doyle, Jack, *op. cit.*
16. Leenders, Hans, 'Reflections on 25 years of service to the international seed trade federation', *Seedsmen's Digest*, 37:5, p. 89.
17. Quoted in Kloppenburg, *op. cit.*, p. 266.
18. *Ibid.*
19. Rural Advancement Foundation International (RAFI), Ottawa, '*Biodiversity, UNCED and GATT*', unpublished document, 1991.
20. RAFI, *ibid.*
21. RAFI, *ibid.*
22. FAO, International Undertaking on Plant Genetic Resources, DOC C83/II REP/4 and 5, 1983, Rome.
23. Keystone International Dialogue on Plant Genetic Resources, 'Final Consensus Report of Third Plenary Session, May 31—June 4, 1991', The Keystone Center, Colorado, US.
24. 'Disclosures: UPOV sells out', GRAIN, Barcelona, Dec 2, 1990.
25. Shiva, Vandana, 'Biodiversity, biotechnology and Bush', Third World Network Earth Summit Briefings, Third World Network, Penang, 1992.
26. Shiva, Vandana, 'GATT and agriculture', *The Observer*, Bombay, 1992.
27. Postman, Neil, *Technology; The Surrender of Culture to Technology*, A. Knopf, USA, 1992.
28. Singer, Peter, and Wells, Deane, *The Reproductive Revolution: New Ways of Making Babies*, Oxford University Press, Oxford, 1984.
29. Chesler, Phyllis, *Sacred Bond: Motherhood Under Siege*, Virago, London, 1988.
30. European Patent Office, Application No. 833075534.
31. Von Werlhof, Claudia, *op. cit.*
32. Waring, Marilyn, *If Women Counted*, Harper & Row, New York, 1988.
33. United Nations Conference on Environment and Development, Agenda 21, adopted by the Plenary on June 14, 1992, published by UNCED Secretariat, Conches, Switzerland.

The Re-greening of the Planet

Rosalie Bertell

On September 1, 1989 many people remembered the fiftieth anniversary of the first act of aggression of World War II when Hitler's army marched into Poland. The Nazis staged a phoney Polish attack on Germany, using prisoners dressed up as Polish soldiers in order to win some German support for the war, and whip up nationalistic feelings about the humiliating and crippling defeat arrangements after World War I. Hitler's appeal to excessive nationalism and pride, together with racial prejudice and economic greed, created a war machine which devoured some 50 million lives and spread human misery from the European death camps to the ravished Pacific Island. The surprising thing about the Hitler phenomenon is the large number of people who cooperated with it: civil engineers who created human incinerators and gas chambers; lower echelon SS troops who ran death camps; scientists who created lethal gases; physicians who experimented on prisoners; masons who walled in the ghettos; transportation workers who managed the death trains.

Over the next few years we will be commemorating every major event of those tragic war years, culminating with the fiftieth anniversary of the brutal fire and carpet bombings of Germany and Japan and the nuclear holocaust of Hiroshima and Nagasaki. In 1996 we can begin to commemorate the beginning of nuclear weapon testing in the Pacific and in the year 2001, fifty years of nuclear destruction of the Nevada desert, Novaya Semlya and Khazikstan.

How have we progressed in stewarding our natural, human and scientific resources for peace over the last forty-four years? I think any impartial witness would describe the forty-four years as an armed truce, with each side increasing its kill power to a mind-boggling extreme. Our natural, human and scientific resources are still heavily engaged in military research, production and activities. True peace would find many major corporations without stable contracts and put thousands of workers out of jobs. High-tech military research departments would have to be dismantled and scientists seek work in civilian research. Clearly society is strongly oriented in the use of natural, human and scientific resources towards war and not towards peace.

We seem to have drifted into this orientation after World War II partly out of old mind-sets and partly because of the shock of nuclear bomb and rocket capability. Nuclear weapon testing began in the Bikini Atoll of the Republic of the Marshall Islands in 1946, even before the U.S. secured this territory. It is the only Trust Territory ever designated, strategic. The Soviets obtained the bomb in 1949, and began testing, as did the British in the 1950s, the French in the 1960s, and India and China in the 1970s. Nuclear testing, now less frequent and currently under a fragile moratorium, is still being carried out or threatened by the French in French Polynesia, by the Americans and the British in Nevada, and by the Russians in Novaya Semlya. Most underground tests release radioactivity into air or water, all release it into soil and rock deposits. The long-lasting radioactive chemicals so produced can migrate to the water table. Nuclear weapon testing has been the epitome of post-World War II misuse of our natural, human and scientific resources. As we assess our ability to redirect these resources towards peace, it is sobering to take a closer look at the true cost of our forty-seven year old armed truce. The second 'stream of death' from World War II, the rockets, are now in ascendancy and their negative effects on world climate are just being realized. We will deal with this topic also.

It has always been surprising to me that the *New York Times* can simultaneously depict the nuclear and space arms race as destroying the economy of the Soviet Union but providing prosperity in North America. The dollar drain into the military has been well publicised, but what about the stress on the environment, the human guinea pigs, and the brain drain? Is militarism as practiced between 1946 and 1993 a human and ecological disaster as well as a misallocation of financial resources?

Another surprising thing is that we assumed the earth could absorb and heal any damage we did to it in the name of national security. How could our survival strategy destroy our life-support systems: our air, water, land and food? It is this stark reality which is turning many hard-nosed business persons into peacenik-environmentalists. However, myth and secrecy still mute the voice of the earth, and the full ravages of fifty years of preparation for nuclear and star wars are only gradually coming to light.

Nuclear weapons begin with uranium mining and milling; uranium occurs in rock together with other radioactive material such as thorium, radium, radon gas, radioactive lead, bismuth and polonium. This mixture is removed from the earth and crushed, making it more bio-available. Most of the radioactive rock is left above ground at the mine site. The waste to uranium ore ratio varies by mine site, but a general low grade mine such as the proposed uranium mine at Baker Lake in the Canadian Northwest Territories is 13 to 1. Only one per cent of mined rock is retrieved from the mill as yellowcake. This means that for every ton of yellowcake (unenriched uranium), 1300 tons of radioactive waste rock are left at the mine and mill sites. Often these sites are on the land of indigenous people.

To produce one Nagasaki type atomic bomb, small by today's standards, one would leave 3.4 tons of radioactive waste at the uranium mine and mill site, 3.5 tons of uranium refinery waste and 0.4 tons of high level spent nuclear fuel waste. There would be an additional large amount of so-called low level radioactive waste resulting from the processing, handling and transportation of this material.

Without even considering the nuclear testing, this 'war effort' has generated a surprising number of casualties. Using industry production figures and United Nations estimates of worker exposure one can make a first estimate of the human cost upto the year 2000, as 90,000 cancers — about 50,000 are in workers and 40,000 in members of the public. This is assuming no accidents or abnormal radiation releases. If we include all of the above-ground nuclear weapon testing, the number of cancers soars to three million; almost all of these are civilian.

But cancers are not the only problem with uranium and nuclear pollution. There are an additional expected two million fetal or infant deaths, 10.4 million children with genetic diseases (this includes Mendelian genetic diseases, chromosome abnormalities and adult onset diseases with a genetic component), and another 10.6 million born with various degrees of mental and physical retardation. This is because radiation damages the sensitive DNA (genetic code) of cells, including sperm and ova, or even the precursor cells of the brain or pituitary gland in a human embryo. Some genetic damage takes two or three generations to become visible.

The total number of so-called peace time human casualties is: 15.4 million fatalities or severe disabilities and an additional 10.6 million with lesser disabilities. Secondary problems related to inability to carry on normally at school or work because of congenital damage from radiation has not been calculated in this number.

There are many secondary and tertiary problems related to the primary phenomenon. We don't 'see' these damages where they are concentrated, in the Marshall Islands, among the aboriginal people of Australia, the Navajo and Dene people of North America, the circumpolar people or the Congolese and Namibians of Africa, because these people are powerless and voiceless within the dominant western patriarchal culture. Where the health problems are less concentrated people are left wondering where or how their cancer or their damaged child originated. For fifty years we have been told no one has ever definitively proved that these health effects have occurred. Meanwhile no large studies have been undertaken by governments or industry and no detailed records of exposure are kept. Rather, governments spend their time trying to discount independent studies demonstrating the problems. Science by non-investigation is fraudulent.

Pollution should not be judged innocent unless caught in the act of killing, apprehended, and identified definitively as its cause. If you discover a dead person with a bullet in his heart you call it murder, even if you cannot identify the murderer. When the bullets become small (and radioactive particles are very much like small bullets exploded at high speeds within the human body) the damage is identifiable and the crime should be named and the murderer more seriously pursued. In a society which develops risk-benefit thinking, the risk always means life and health, the benefit always means economic, material or political gain. Once one has made the trade-off, one tries to convince everyone, especially the victims, that the decision is rational. Rarely does government or industry measure the casualties to document the risk. This only brings down liability claims or shows up their original underestimation. Only after much debate and prodding by independent scientists did the U.S. government admit in 1987 its underestimation of atomic bomb cancers in Japan. The exposure levels have not yet been changed to reflect the errors admitted and many of us believe the admission of error is not yet full.

Based on a very rough yet conservative assumption that there are 50,000 thermonuclear bombs in the global arsenal, one could estimate, on average, that 520 casualties are caused with each unused bomb in the global nuclear stockpile. These deaths are the cost of deterrence and could be prevented by switching to a peace-oriented society.

Mind altering drugs were used in deliberate brain-washing experiments in the 1960s. Some of the drugs, such as LSD, became major street problems and even posed problems of substance abuse within the armed forces. Many human guinea pigs still suffer the effects of these human experiments which constituted an incredible misuse of human and scientific resources.

Missile testing continues the legacy of death and disability. Large missile testing programmes, such as the MX, include catapulting dummy warheads filled with uranium into Pacific lagoons. The force of impact breaks up the coral, providing a breeding ground for a small dynaflagelites which, if eaten by fish, causes ciguatera fish poisoning in humans. This extremely painful and violent poisoning often results in death or a lifetime inability to eat fish. This is disastrous on a tropical island where fish is the main protein.

Pesticides, herbicides and defoliants were military inventions for killing the tropical jungle in Vietnam, that have caused devastating damage to the people of Vietnam, the American military who fought there, and even to the residents of the Love Canal who found the toxic residue from the production of these chemicals bubbling up in their gardens and basements.

In Vietnam, the vegetation, living plants and trees which provided cover for 'the enemy' were poisoned. Great areas of farmland and tropical forest were completely wiped out by 'trigger factors' such as Agent Orange which kills trees by stripping them of leaves first. Because of the interdependence between animals and plants, animals not directly poisoned were starved to death. One spraying of Agent Orange was sufficient to destroy great areas of mangroves, which in turn resulted in local loss of many animal species and even of species of fish which rely on nutrients flowing from the mangrove vegetation into the surrounding waterways. In humans, the most devastating damage was to the embryo in its mother's womb. It is estimated that one million Vietnamese were poisoned between 1966 and 1969.

The prestigious U.S. Midwest Research Institute summed up the devastation for the military by saying: 'The presence of toxic residues on rice from spraying fields appears not to be a problem since no rice develops in these fields.' The commercial spin-offs of this military activity have caused numerous problems for farms globally and spawned thousands of toxic waste dumps in North America. Chemical farming is credited with unprecedented loss of farm top soil in the U.S.

When one examines the major environmental problems — acid rain, ozone depletion, climate change, loss of top soil, forest die-back, desertification and loss of tropical rainforests — one sees that these earth-illnesses have resulted in loss of species, increases in human allergies, asthmas and cancers, and an increase in congenitally damaged children. If one stays only in the civilian sector when looking for environmental culprits, one finds fossil fuel generators, CFCs from refrigerators and air conditioners, automobiles, sewage and garbage disposal, plastic wrappings, etc. The 'remedy' lies in the 3 R strategy: reduce, reuse and recycle, combined with legislation to reduce emissions. Individuals are counselled to not smoke, not eat fatty foods and not sit in the sun.

Let's look at the military reality.

Acid rain: Did you know that nuclear explosions (and also emissions from nuclear generators) inject electrons (beta particles) into the air causing interactions with nitrogen, oxygen and water vapour, to produce nitrates and nitric acid? The shift in the northern hemisphere's pH due to some 500 atmospheric nuclear explosions and 433 nuclear generators had never been estimated or even mentioned in the acid rain debate. Once the pH is reduced from seven to five the earth's ecosystem becomes vulnerable to every slight change in the acidity of rain. Preparation for nuclear war was probably a prominent component of the acid rain crisis which threatens our lakes, fish, trees and our own respiratory tracts.

Ozone destruction: In the 1950s commercial use of supersonic aircraft was curtailed because of research that showed it would damage the ozone layer. This did not deter the military which routinely uses supersonic planes. The space shuttle alone dumps 75 tonnes of chlorine directly into the ozone layer every time it is sent up. The enlarged rocket motor used in the June 1992 flight with its enhanced boosters, probably released even more. Deliberate military experiments conducted out of Churchill, Manitoba involve chemical release modules. Some of the chemicals used, for example barium chlorates, sodium and magnesium, are known to damage the ozone. All solid fuel rockets whether for testing cruise missiles, transcontinental missiles or anti-scuds used in war, damage the ozone layer because they emit large amounts of hydrochloric acid. These emissions are a part of the global budget of atmospheric destruction and should not be exempted from scrutiny. During the 1980s there were on average 500 to 600 rockets launched yearly, reaching a peak in 1989 (prior to the Gulf War) of 1500 launches.

Climate change: The problems of climate change include both a nuclear winter scenario and a greenhouse effect. Prior to the Gulf War many scientists warned of a 'nuclear winter' effect if the Iraqi oil wells were torched. After the fact, with an extraordinarily cool summer in North America and an equally abnormally cool spring in Japan and the Pacific, our newspapers place all the blame on Mt. Pinatubo in the Philippines. Certainly both have some effect but why are we silent about the military contribution? Why do we claim air exchange in the upper atmosphere between the northern and southern hemisphere, when the Gulf War requires no such postulated exchange? Very little is also said about the respiratory illnesses in our military who fought in the Gulf and breathed the toxic fumes. We have no updates on the oil spills and resultant depletion of fish stock or impact on desalination plants. What about the destruction of the fragile desert ecosystem? What about the two nuclear reactors and high level nuclear waste which was exploded by allied bombs? What about the use of uranium tanks for the first time and subsequent illness of the men who rode in them?

Czechoslovakian retired meteorologist, Mr. Forchtgott, who used to work at a military air base at Mosnov, Northern Moravia, recorded changes in climate and meteorological conditions due to nuclear power plants. The Dukovany and Bohunice nuclear generators release 3.5 cubic meters of hot water every second into the atmosphere. A 'smog river', 20-30 kms wide moves north into the heavy industry, dust-polluted area of Northern Moravia. The hot air takes up most of the water in the atmosphere, carries it north, cools, allowing the water to condense on the dust particles, causing heavy destructive rain over small areas and decreased rain in large areas. The 'smog river' is visible from satellite.

Greenhouse: At the greenhouse end of the climate spectrum, the primary culprit identified is carbon dioxide. The nuclear industry would like you to think that shifting to nuclear power and phasing out fossil fuel generators would solve the problem. Did you know that the carbon dioxide emission of commercial jet planes is 30 times more effective than the same amount emitted on earth? Military flights which are another 20,000 ft. higher than commercial flights may have an efficiency of 100 times.

In addition to these more obvious problems, the NASA Technical Paper 1750 states: 'Historically, chemical releases have been conducted for scientific studies from several hundred sounding rockets over the past 25 years. Similar releases have been conducted from several orbiting vehicles at large distances from earth.' NASA admits that some of its experiments triggered auroras or substorms with geomagnetic activity. It is to be remembered that although NASA is the civilian space agency in the U.S. it cooperates with military space experiments. Military activities both in the U.S. and USSR are secret for reasons of national security. These programmes have little or no civilian accountability even with today's heightened environmental awareness. There are about 5,000 satellites in orbit around the earth and some 11,000 pieces of space debris large enough to be detected by radar.

Surrogate wars: While the subject of the environmental and human costs of the armed truce since 1945 are huge and only briefly touched upon here, they pale against a background of surrogate wars for spheres of influence in the economically developing countries. There have been at least another 25 million deaths in these so-called low level conflicts in Africa, Asia and Latin America.

Non-military oriented economics: It is possible to manage our natural, human and scientific resources for peace: Perhaps until recently, Japan and West Germany were the best examples of non-military-oriented societies. Their bright young people devoted their scientific minds to civilian electronics and automobiles, running away with the world markets. Internationally, the countries with the strongest commitment to social programmes have generally had weaker commitments to militarism. A good example is Costa Rica which has no army.

It will be important as we reach the year 2000 to reflect on post-World War II military economy, to make visible the self-destructive nature of the armed truce it spawned and the real need for conversion to a global peace society. This need is at the level of survival of the human race and its life-supporting habitat.

Neither choice, survival or destruction, happens by magic — each is built up by millions of small deliberate actions leading one way or the other. We can see clearly that both trends are developing within our countries and it is essential to distinguish which one we are reinforcing. The unthinking person today endangers all of us on this fragile earth, because the unthinking repeat outmoded behaviour even when it becomes self-destructive.

Can women, united internationally, provide millions of centres of clarity, dialogue, conflict resolution and good will to move the global agenda towards a sustainable and peace-oriented global community? That is the hope which brought us together in Miami (1991) and Rio de Janeiro (1992). This is the outcome whose sustaining energy brings us to hope in a new and different future. The great task of an even-handed, systematic dismantling of the war machines of East and West, North and South must be undertaken.

When we pose the topic, managing our natural, human and scientific resources for peace we have already admitted that we are dealing with a human behaviour problem:

'managing our oceans' can mean wisely limiting fishing so as to maximise aquatic quality and balance, ensuring a food supply for all; or it can mean staking our territorial rights and being ready to destroy the planet if anyone disregards our claim. It can mean using our resources to enhance and improve fish habitats, or dumping our toxic waste in the seas.

'managing human resources' can mean developing the gentler humanising arts together with skills in conflict resolution and rules of harmonious living within a strained biosphere; or it can mean skimming off the brightest young people to move into high-paid secret war industries to refine production of megadeath. It can mean open and democratic government or rule by force, intimidation, lying and torture.

'managing scientific resources' can mean improving the quality of life and health of the most impoverished nations; sharing of ideas; improving communication; freedom of mobility and choice; or it can mean high-tech concentration of surveillance techniques and instruments of terror so as to consolidate money and power among a privileged few.

Our task is to deliberately choose our behaviour so as to harmonise with our earth life-support system, cooperate with our human counterparts in a global community and implement nonviolent ways to reach just resolutions of the inevitable conflicting self-interests which will arise. Change of behaviour depends heavily on change of perception. Perception requires reflection, self-praise and self-criticism, and incredible courage.

In times of change we are all on a ship being propelled in one direction. Some of the people are aft-looking, backward and trying to hold on to past behaviour; some of them are forward, straining to see the future and learning new behaviour so as to be ready; and the bureaucrats are in the middle pretending nothing is happening. The most important truths are that we are not alone and we cannot stay where we are. We can choose only to look forward or backward; we can close our eyes or we can be fully alive and awake to our reality.

Our basic understanding of our dilemma will need to be revised. The past fifty years have witnessed a clear confrontational polarisation between capitalism and communism. These are really two different priority systems around which the economy can be organized. If I can be allowed to caricature a bit, capitalism has money as its bottom line: efficiency, production and economic survival drive the wheels. In communism, the bottom line is ideology even if ideological purity calls for inefficiency and financial waste. Today we see both systems perpetrating the same damage to the earth life support system, the same misdirection of scientific and human resources, although fortunately for us, both systems are softening under the strain. I believe the future pathway will have a common bottom line acceptable to both capitalism and communism; namely survival of life on earth as we now know it. This transcends all other differences and priorities.

Is women's traditional work of raising and educating future leaders governed by a desire to move the social agenda towards the future or is it merely reproducing the most noticeable faults of the old behaviour pattern? Do women's choices make visible the undesirable elements in the war system and move the perception of people towards the peace system? If they do not pass the test of future making, then they are reinforcing the status quo and thereby assisting the movement of the global community (by default) into the logical outcome of nation-state sovereignty and war behaviour, namely ecological disaster and collapse of all civilization. During the fifty years of armed truce since World War II men have created hydrogen bombs a thousand times more devastating than the Hiroshima bomb together with many other chemical and biological agents to finish off one small planet. We have also created a global climate of competition and anti-survival behaviour. We have failed miserably at giving our children any hope of a world without war. In fact, we have taught them that war is inevitable and little boys playing with guns is 'normal'.

Perhaps 'management' is too active a word, but certainly responsible stewardship of our global natural, human and scientific resources can reduce fear and conflict and create a stable environment for peace and biological well-being. Maybe with collaboration the art of womanagement could be invented.

One major area of analysis relative to the formation of a global community is that of energy production and distribution. This topic very obviously interacts with environmental questions and militarism. How, as energy consumers and citizens, can we begin to make global survival of a viable biosphere the bottom line of our energy choices? During the last fifty years, energy choices have been dominated by military research.

The food chain is also a basic survival focus, clearly related to degradation of air, water and land, as well as to climate changes, political uses of food and severe malnutrition and starvation. Wars have been fought over access to food and secure food supply is the basic underpinning of any global peace plan. In the past, water has been undervalued, polluted, and even used as a theatre for naval wars. Can a fragile global community continue to do this with impunity? What are the implications for war and peace inherent in our life on the water planet earth?

Underlying the paradigm switch from economics and ideology as bottom lines is the realization that we live within a delicately balanced, already well designed ecosphere. 'Managing' becomes less relevant than understanding and respecting. Manipulating gives way to the art of harmonising. How does this insight become incorporated into social behaviour appropriate to the aspirations of the global community?

What is being proposed is a major re-greening of the planet, marked by a shift away from all forms of militarism into a viable and sustainable global living system. The agenda calls for a critical re-evaluation of the fifty year remembrances of World War II and its sequellae. Women can help make visible the victims of the last fifty years: radiation victims in the Pacific Islands, Arctic and weapon testing sites; the atomic and Agent Orange veterans and their victims; the native people whose land and lives have been ravaged; the developing countries seeking their own place in the sun, caught in 'super power' conflicts.

Just as we measure economic failure by poverty and unemployment, and ideological failure by political dissent, so too we must gauge our success in creating a peaceful world by the promotion of and the will to commit violence. In the midst of a world eager for technological crumbs from the table of military priorities, women can strike out for civilian based research and sustainable solutions. This might not be an immediate economic benefit, but survival depends on it. Again the key shift is towards survival as the bottom line.

The years ahead may be rocky and full of tension. Even today as governments laud almost fifty years of peace, the governed take to the streets in unprecedented numbers to demand peace because the reality is war. In a time of unparalleled wealth and technological capability we have mass starvation in Ethiopia and Somalia, millions undernourished or living on the streets in North America, and children choosing crack or suicide out of an illusory life of glitter and false values. Our reality is a highly armed truce — not peace.

The choices are real. They are hard. They will be rewarding if we have the courage to grasp them. Every person, every talent is required for the behaviour shift to become a reality. Our lives, our habits, our possessions, our fears, our prejudices are all touched and challenged. The only ones who feel overwhelmed and paralysed at the impossibility of the task are those who have never tried to help. Those who have begun the task of shaping the future could use a million helpers to do the million things needed for a smooth transition. Fifty years from now will see the celebration of the lives of those who had the courage to dismantle the war mentality and build up the peace mentality. In September 2039, will the global celebration remember a hundred years of war or fifty years of peace conversion? It will take all of us together to dismantle the war mentality, strengthen courts and international peace-keeping, learn conflict resolution, heal the wounds of the past and bring about the re-greening of this stupendously beautiful planet earth.

I would like to close with an excerpt from a prophetic speech by Chief Seattle, delivered in 1854 when he surrendered Indian land, now called the State of Washington, to the U.S. government:

The shining water that moves in the streams and rivers is not just water, but the blood of our ancestors. If we sell you our land, you must remember that it is sacred and you must teach your children that it is sacred . . . The rivers are our brothers, they quench our thirst . . . The air is precious to the red man, for all things share the same breath — the beast, the tree, the man, they all share the same breath . .

This we know. The earth does not belong to man: man belongs to the earth. This we know. All things are connected like the blood which unites one family. All things are connected.

Whatever befalls the earth befalls the sons of the earth. Man did not weave the web of life; he is merely a strand in it. Whatever he does to the web, he does to himself . . . The white man too shall pass; perhaps sooner than all other tribes. Continue to contaminate your beds, and you will one night suffocate in your own waste.

Notes

1. Rosalie Bertell, *No Immediate Danger: Prognosis for a Radioactive Earth,* London: The Women's Press, 1985.
2. Rosalie Bertell, *Handbook for Estimating the Health Effects from Exposure to Ionizing Radiation,* Toronto: IICPH, 1986.
3. WISE News Communique 382, Amsterdam, November 20, 1992.
4. *Nature,* January 1992.
5. Rosalie Bertell, 'Destruction of the Environment, a Living Biosphere,' in Daniel Leviton, (ed.) *Horrendous Death, Health and Well-being,* New York: Hemisphere Publishing Co., 1991.
6. Rosalie Bertell, "Estimate of Uranium and Nuclear Radiation Casualties Attributable to Activities since 1945," *Medicine and War* 4: 27–36, 1988.

Ecological Economics*

Marilyn Waring

Most of what I have to say is what I would consider common sense, taught to me by generations of women, so I don't think it's going to be too complicated. But just a few brief basics, first. The boys are calling a whole new field of study 'ecological economics' — it's a bit of a problem with 'eco-', derived from the Greek 'home'. The way the boys treat ecological economics doesn't have a great deal to do with home. It's almost a contradiction in terms, if you can imagine it, because it uses conventional economic tools despite all the caveats which the boys enter about how these are not really appropriate and it's very difficult to cram them all into one system, and so on. For those of you who aren't up with the play, 'growth' is productivity, it's anything that passes through the market, for which cash is exchanged. There isn't a debit side to growth so it's not like running the housekeeping and there isn't a legal or illegal demarcation. So it's really good for growth to smoke lots of cigarettes, have lots of car accidents, and wars are sensational. I don't know why people worry about Noriega. Illegal drugs are what a lot of the South produces to even get any form of growth rate.

So growth and productivity are basically interchangeable. One of the real crimes of the colonisation of a perfectly good language which economics is engaged in, has meant that development now has come to be synonymous with growth. And they've been used together in such cliche forms that I'm not sure it's very useful to us to pursue the word 'development' any more and to think that we can contextually lift it from its cliched abandonment to 'growth'. Also it's perfectly obvious in terms of the development that a lot of us speak about that you can improve the quality of life without spending any money, and that that probably has a lot more to do with sustainability than anything that passes through the market.

Now there's another word that has real problems and that's the word 'value', because the moment you speak about it in terms of ecological economics it's seen as an expression of a shadow price. In spite of the fact that it's a wonderfully good word — its Latin derivation is from *valore*

*Testimony by Marilyn Waring of New Zealand at the World Women's Congress for a Healthy Planet, Miami, USA, November 10, 1991.

which means to be strong, to be worthy — most of us hear the word now in its economic market context and, environmentally, it's seen to be an expression of individualistic human preferences. To give you an example of what that means, when the Environment Protection Agency (EPA) in this country are trying to decide, 'What is the value of this river? Shall we dam it or not?' one of the tools that they use is called WFUD which stands for 'wildlife fish-user days'. And so part of the value of the river is how many fishing licenses do you think you could sell and how many fish do you think they might catch. And this is the kind of shadow price and the expression of individualistic human preferences that is being used in ecological economics.

Now the very first textbook of this has just been written by old bright boys who have been getting themselves published in journals as mavericks, interestingly enough, for about the last ten or fifteen years.* I brought it along so we could all have a look at it — it has three women and forty-two men in it, and apart from one Brazilian, they're all from the US or Europe, and six are from the World Bank. The Conference was funded by the World Bank and USAID and it says things like, 'To achieve sustainability we must incorporate ecosystem goods and services into our economic accounting. The first step is to determine values for them comparable to those economic goods and services.' Now this is the general tenor of the commentary despite, as I say, loads of caveats.

Herman Daley adjusted US GNP to account for the depletions in natural capital, pollution effects and income distribution, and the results of those studies show that in the last twenty-five years there's been no growth whatever in the United States, just a running down of the inventory of natural capital. When I say they enter the caveats, this is important because we need to use some of these voices sometimes for our own needs. So they talk about the old framework of national income accounting being mechanistic and atomistic. They say that it lacks any representation of materials, of energy sources, of physical structures, of time-dependent processes that are basic to an ecological approach. Now where this leads them is to say that we have to develop economic accounting systems that reflect physical conductivity and positive feedback dynamics such as you find in biological systems. Anyone familiar with economics and mathematics will see that these boys are going to keep themselves in business for a very long time . . . bigger models, with feedbacks, and they even have debit sides. When you read *Ecological Economics* you feel as if you are reading chapter after chapter of various curriculum vitae for the big new business in the courts and in multinationals and in country after

* Robert Constanza (ed.), *Ecological Economics*, New York: Columbia University Press 1991

country, of my model is bigger, better and brighter than your model.

Let me give you a an example: they started talking about 'carrying' capacity. Well, I am a farmer, quite a genuine farmer—and they go on about 'carrying capacity' and say, 'Carrying capacity is now something we're going to use to determine what flows need to be *managed* and *controlled*.' So the three flows which must be *managed* and *controlled* in terms of carrying capacity are 'materials, energy, and people'. So, 'there are simple non-interfering instruments to control the first two, for example, energy taxes, severance taxes, and other virgin material taxes. These taxes are special forms of excise taxes and are simple to collect . . .' and so on and on about taxes. Then they say,

It is more difficult to identify instruments to control population with minimal interference and high leverage. Thus it is reported that the most successful programmes in India are those which involve the education of women. Educational programmes lower the birth rates in three ways: they postpone the time of family formation, they encourage women to enter the formal sector economy and they increase the family decision power of women who tend to want smaller families than men.

You see this is all written as though it were a revelation to these chaps! But wait, there's more:

Given that education is generally considered good social policy for reasons other than population control, education programmes, which coincidentally lower birth rates are likely to be more acceptable than other population programmes many of which are indirectly coercive. A second alternative is also non-coercive: at the level of the individual parent, it works by increasing freedoms at least for the parents. The technology of sex selection is made available to prospective parents and they are allowed to choose their children's sex. In some countries, this possibility of choice can have a profound effect on both the birth rate and the sex ratio. In countries with strong preferences towards male children there will be a smaller proportion of girls. While this policy alternative may be effective in lowering birth rates now, in a generation from now policy people are understandably concerned that it might have disruptive effects and so they are cautious about it.

What is alarming to me is that the reason we have to be cautious about it is because it might have disruptive policy effects! This to me is outrageous. The third alternative they say is old age. The reason I quote this little bit especially in the context of carrying capacity and as a farmer, is because one knows that if one is overstocked, the first basic rule is that you kill the males you don't need for breeding. So I think that if these chaps want to run around lifting metaphors from us illiterate peasants, they better know what carrying capacity is all about.

Now let me talk about some of the other things they get into or are already doing. One of the ideas they have is called the substitution of natural capital. Now the idea of this is that you can drain the wetland as long as you build us an artificial one to replace it. One of the gentlemen in this book seriously raises the question, 'How could we replace the radiation screening services of the ozone layer currently being destroyed?

One of the things that we should note about all this is that it involves attributing a market price to everything we're talking about. So they may talk about intergenerational equity — well, it's always wonderful to hear the boys who brought you the problem bringing you the solution. They don't seem to know a lot about equity here and now so I don't have a great deal of confidence in their delivering us intergenerational equity. But also it seems to presume that there is already a good enough resource base to hand on, as if somehow or other the mess that we've made is a satisfactory inheritance, as if all we have to do is keep the capital intact to hand on to the next generation.

They also say when they talk about intergenerational equity (and equity always makes me nervous when it comes out of the mouth of a white man) that this prediction does not depend on the identity of any particular individuals — that sentence in a phrase about equity is hair-raising.

Then the other things they go with: one of the new ones is 'environmental insurance bonding'; and companies are going to be asked to post bonds to 'the current best estimate of the largest potential future environmental damages,' and the money will be kept in interest-bearing accounts, and the bond is returned in thirty years when the firm now can prove that there's been no damage . . . The whole notion of forseeability is involved here or, if we reflect on what some of the major environmental or health hazards have been . . . what you see is that things that couldn't have been anticipated at the time the 'current estimate' was made, then it doesn't look as if you're going to be required to pay anything out of your insurence bond. So that's another little trick they put up their sleeves.

One of my favourites is 'the tradeable pollution quotas, the tradeable emission standards'. Everybody gets the right to pollute just this much — every individual and every factory and every country, apparently. This started off by saying, obviously there's too much pollution in the air so we'll pop around all the factories and we'll license everybody . . . We'll decide what a level of fresh air is (obviously this level of fresh air was designed for people with no asthma, no bronchial disorders, no lung problems) and then we'll set the ceiling and then we'll license every industry to pollute up to this ceiling. These become tradeable emission quotas so that if I've got a really grubby factory and someone else has got a really clean factory, she can sell me the permission to put into the air all the pollution that she doesn't, and that way we can make the standard. Now this is hot-footing it right across the United States as a 'wonderful' policy and the deputy director of the EPA thinks that this is a godsend for the South. So every country gets to put this much pollution into the air and those countries in my region like Tonga and Samoa and Vanuatu and the Cook and people who don't actually have a great deal of industrial production (and don't even have 67 million sheep, bcause we have a major flatulence problem in New Zealand in terms of the ozone layer and depletion) they'll be able to sell their emission quotas to the North, or to other countries in our region like Thailand that has deeply troublesome pollution standards.

Then, of course, there are fees and taxes and revenues and there's discounting, where you try to work out what return on forgone present consumption can be sacrificed to insure future consumption. Then there are depreciation calculations and all of this, of course, is done with things like computer models.

One of the things that really bothers me, and that I understand very well in terms of being a past policy maker is this : when you're desperate to save something, whether it's a river, an ecosystem, a forest, you think you're ready to use whatever tools can immediately empower you or give your argument power. And it's very, very tempting to think that since economics is all powerful, the way in which we can empower our beloved ecosystem is to give it a monetary value — quantify it. I used to think that, especially when I was in parliament, mostly because I desperately had to prove that mountains and forests had any value at all. It will not, of course, generally have escaped your notice that there are only three things left out of the market around the world: leisure (I couldn't work that out for years. I couldn't see why it was a problem to leave leisure out, and the reason I couldn't work it out was because I never had any and the men did and they couldn't bear that there was a part of their lives that was unaccounted for, so they had to note that leisure didn't count), environmental degradation, the free gift of nature and all unpaid work of women — all are left out of national income accounting.

There is no economic instrument which can adequately attribute market value to any part of the ecosystem or to any part of the ecosystem function. Now that leaves us with a pretty difficult question because we must fight what is happening very hard. The United Nations statistical office has already approved the establishment of environmental accounts inside the system of national accounts. These are going to operate as satellite. They will involve the commodification of everything that can be perceived as having a market value. But these things are nightmares, because national income accounting works inside nation-states and one of the things that nature can teach us, thankfully, is that it doesn't know anything about nation-state boundaries. Now is acid rain going to be recorded as a natural export to Canada? And where is Canada going to record this in its income account? The same for Norway: is it just going to think that it got some aid from the UK when the next bit of acid rain hits? Where is it supposed to pop it? And in the Pacific when the French just exploded another bomb in Munuroa and we would just have liked to send it home to Paris. When we get our jellyfish babies and our leukaemia, just where are we supposed to record this in our national income accounts? When multinational pharmaceutical companies like Sandoz pour all kinds of muck into the Rhine in Switzerland, does the pollution stop at the Swiss border — does it say, 'Not me, I'm made in Switzerland, I'll just stop right here.' The ecosystem doesn't seem to know about nation-state boundaries. The possibility that we think we own fish is always a great laugh to me, everybody running around sort of cutting up the ocean and giving out fishing quotas and 200-mile zones. There must be amazing fish down there, they've all got glasses and they all know where the boundaries are.

So I have some trouble with the fact that we think we can number-crunch it inside a nation-state context. But the inability to attribute a market value to some part of the ecosystem doesn't mean that it's not worthy of consideration. The treatment of the environment in national accounts and in public policy reproduces the arrogant ideology that only money is of value—only the market is a source of knowledge. It suggests that all of life can be condensed to this narrow and soulless view. From a feminist perspective, none of those advocating sustainable development address the indicators or suggest that development is any less dependent on economic growth than the current exploitative market. It seems to me to be just a play with words. The heart of the problem is avoided in a diligent bow to patriarchal power.

Another reason why this really troubles me, and it's never said out loud and frequently enough, is that as long as the market rolls and we try to impute values to the ecosystem, the graft and corruption and politics around the planet is of such magnitude that if we could isolate it in national income accounting a lot of people could live off it for years. I don't want to pretend that it's not in the interest of a number of countries in my region of the world to actually see the ecosystem imputed into national income accounts, because then the payoff into the Swiss bank accounts when the big policies come in will be even larger. There are, I think, major ways in which we can look at valuations and let me just run through a couple of those. There are the measure of the state of the natural environment, air, water and soil, by repeated monitoring of changes in that state. These measures have been made for a long time. There are the measures of the quantities of discharge of substances regarded as pollutants. There is the measure of the consequences of pollution for human health, for animal, bird and marine life, and for plant contamination. The final thing I want to say is that I think we're running headlong for market indicators because that's the source of patriarchal power. It's the source of the knowledge, it keeps us out of the argument; it's an argument carried on in an obscure language which means that the majority of the people can't participate. It's very simple for cowardly politicians to make decisions simply by trying to indicate whether the growth rate is going up or down. It means they never have to exercise judgement about anything; it means they never have to exercise themselves about being informed. I actually believe that all the moves that are being heralded in things like the UNCED document towards environmental or ecological accounting are a nightmare; that they urge us even further towards values of pathological destructiveness. I don't want to see the things I love appearing in national income accounts, called valuable along with nuclear bombs, nuclear power stations, toxic waste, female sexual slavery, trade in drugs, and everything else. That is the invitation that is being extended to us and we ought to turn it down right now.

Notes on Contributors

Loreta B. Ayupan started organising peasant women in South Cotabato, Mindanao in the late Seventies. She helped found BUGAS, the peasant women's organisation of South Cotabato, and the local affiliate of AMIHAN in the area. Persistent organising work among the poor women in Mindanao made her an 'undesirable element' in the eyes of the military and an arrest order was issued on her person. She is currently one of the honorary chairpersons of AMIHAN. She is also a member of the National Consultative Council of the GABRIELA National Women's Coalition.

Rosalie Bertell health and environmental activist, is the author of numerous articles and papers on these issues, including the seminal *No Immediate Danger: Prognosis for a Radioactive Earth.* She is Director of the International Institute of Concern for Public Health (Canada).

The Forum Against Sex Determination and Sex Pre-selection is an organisation of concerned activists from women's and people's science groups in Bombay, who have been working consistently on women's health issues, particularly on contraception, fertility and reproductive rights.

Indira Jaising is a senior advocate who practises in the Supreme Court of India. She is Founder and Secretary of the Lawyers' Collective, an organisation which provides legal aid and assistance to the underprivileged. She is editor of *the Lawyers,* a monthly journal on law and social justice, published from Bombay since 1986. She has provided legal services to victims of the Bhopal gas tragedy.

Penny Newman's professional training is as a speech and language pathologist. In September 1986 she left teaching to become the full-time staff person for Concerned Neighbors in Action. She joined the staff of the Citizens Clearinghouse for Hazardous Wastes, a national environmental organisation, as their western field organiser in 1988 and maintains that position to date. Her job includes helping community-based groups articulate their own issues and develop the skills and tools to empower themselves to fight for and win a clean, healthy environment for themselves and their children. She has published widely on these issues in numerous journals and periodicals.

Teresita G. Oliveros is the deputy secretary-general of AMIHAN, National Federation of Peasant Women. She also heads the national office which provides support to the programmes and projects of the 22 provincial chapters of AMIHAN all over the Philippines. She has been in development work for the past 15 years, organising and helping peasants and fisherfolk build their own organisations in the provinces of northern Philippines.

Gail Omvedt has worked with the Indian women's movement since 1975, in particular with agricultural labour, peasant and tribal women. She was active in organising a national women's conference in Bihar in 1988 and has been part of the Shetkari Mahila Aghadi since its beginning. Her publications include, besides numerous academic and journalistic articles, *Cultural Revolt in a Colonial Society* (1976); *We Will Smash this Prison: Indian Women in Struggle* (1979); *Women in Popular Movements: India and Thailand in the Decade of Women* (1986); *Women Workers in the Unorganized Sector* (1988) and *Violence Against Women: New Movements and New Theories in India* (1990). A major study of the farmers', women's, environmental, and anti-caste movements in India is forthcoming, *Reinventing Revolution: India's New Social Movements.*

C. Sathyamala is a doctor, activist and researcher who has worked with women's groups and in the area of public health. Her current work is on the subject of epidemiology. She provided important inputs into the litigation on behalf of the victims of the Bhopal gas tragedy, and has co-authored two books, *Against All Odds* (1990), and *Taking Sides* (1987), both on alternative health practice.

Rita Sebastian is a well-known freelance journalist in Sri Lanka, who has followed the ethnic conflict in her country since its inception. Her articles have been widely published both in her own country and in the international press. She is also the author of a collection of short stories, *The Night of the Devil Bird.*

Mira Shiva is one of India's best-known health activists, actively associated with the Drug Action Network on issues related to the Indian government's drugs and pharmaceuticals policies. Author of several papers on health, environment and women's issues she is currently Head of the Public Policy Division, Voluntary Health Association of India.

Vandana Shiva well-known environmental activist, physicist and philosopher of science, is Director of the Research Foundation for Science, Technology and Natural Resource Policy, Dehradun. She is the author of *Staying Alive* (1988) *The Violence of the Green Revolution* (1990), *Ecology and the Politics of Survival* (1991) and *Monocultures of the Mind* (1992).

Ann Danaiya Usher has been writing on environmental politics and health issues in Thailand since 1987 as a staff reporter at *The Nation,* an English-language daily newspaper in Bangkok.

Marilyn Waring teaches political science at the University of Waikato, New Zealand. A parliamentarian for twenty years, she now runs a sheep farm in New Zealand, is the Convenor of Sisterhood is Global, lectures and writes, and is the author of the highly acclaimed, *If Women Counted.*

Index